Praise for HUNDREDS OF HEADS™ *Surviv* D1143788

"Hundreds of Heads is an innovative publishing house…its entertain-ing and informative 'How To Survive…' series takes a different approach to offering advice. Thousands of people around the nation were asked for their firsthand experiences and real-life tips in six of life's arenas. Think 'Chicken Soup' meets 'Zagats,' says a press release, and rightfully so."

—ALLEN O. PIERLEONI, "BETWEEN THE LINES," THE SACRAMENTO BEE

"A concept that will be . . . a huge seller and a great help to people. I firmly believe that today's readers want sound bytes of information, not tomes. Your series will most definitely be the next 'Chicken Soup.'"

—CYNTHIA BRIAN
TV/RADIO PERSONALITY, BEST SELLING AUTHOR: CHICKEN SOUP FOR THE GARDENER'S SOUL; BE THE STAR YOU ARE!; THE BUSINESS OF SHOW BUSINESS

"Move over, 'Dummies'. . . Can that 'Chicken Soup!' Hundreds of Heads are on the march to your local bookstore!"

—ELIZABETH HOPKINS,
KFNX (PHOENIX) RADIO HOST, THINKING OUTSIDE THE BOX

Praise for other titles in the HUNDREDS OF HEADS™ *Survival Guide series:*

HOW TO LOSE 9,000 LBS. (OR LESS)

"Informative and entertaining… a must-read if you have ever struggled with the delicate 'D' word."

—ZORA ANDRICH
REALITY SHOW CONTESTANT

"For all of those people who say they've 'been there, done that' when it comes to dieting—this book actually goes there and does that, to show us how to be successful in our own quest for permanent weight loss."

—SUSIE GALVEZ
BEAUTY INDUSTRY EXPERT AND AUTHOR; LOST 120 LBS.

HOW TO SURVIVE YOUR TEENAGER

"Parents of teens and parents of kids approaching those years will find wisdom on each page...provides insight, humor, and empathy..."
—FOREWORD MAGAZINE, *JULY/AUGUST 2005*

"These anecdotes, written by people who have been there, hit the nail on the head! Some you'll recognize as wonderful suggestions or insightful descriptions of true-life experiences. Others will help you recognize traps to avoid. This book tells it like it is."
—STEVEN PERLOW, PH.D.
CLINICAL PSYCHOLOGIST, ATLANTA, GEORGIA

"With warmth, humor and 'I've been there' compassion, editors Gluck and Rosenfeld have turned the ordinary experiences and struggles of parents into bits of compact wisdom that are easy to pick up and use straightaway. I especially liked this book's many examples of how to survive (and even thrive) while living under the same roof as your teen."
—JACLYNN MORRIS, M.ED.
CO-AUTHOR OF I'M RIGHT. YOU'RE WRONG. NOW WHAT? *AND* FROM ME TO YOU

HOW TO SURVIVE YOUR FRESHMAN YEAR

"This book proves that all of us are smarter than one of us."
—JOHN KATZMAN
FOUNDER AND CEO, PRINCETON REVIEW

"Voted in the Top 40 Young Adults books."
—PENNSYLVANIA SCHOOL LIBRARIANS ASSOCIATION

"This cool new book...helps new college students get a head start on having a great time and making the most of this new and exciting experience."
—COLLEGE OUTLOOK

"This book is right on the money. I wish I had this before I started college."
—KATIE LEVITT
SENIOR, GEORGE WASHINGTON UNIVERSITY

HOW TO SURVIVE DATING

"Rated one of the Top 10 Dating Books."

—ABOUT.COM

"Invaluable advice... If I had read this book before I made my movie, it would have been only *10 Dates*."

—MYLES BERKOWITZ, FILMMAKER. WROTE, DIRECTED AND WENT OUT ON 20 DATES FOR FOX SEARCHLIGHT

"Great, varied advice, in capsule form, from the people who should know—those who've dated and lived to tell the tale."

—SALON.COM

"Hilarious!"

—TEENA JONES
THE TEENA JONES SHOW, *KMSR-AM (DALLAS)*

HOW TO SURVIVE A MOVE

"As a realtor, I see the gamut of moving challenges. This book is great - covering everything from a 'heads-up' on the travails of moving to suggested solutions for the problems. AND... it's a great read!"

—JEANNE MOELLENDICK, RE/MAX SPECIALISTS, JACKSONVILLE, FLORIDA

"How to Survive A Move is full of common sense ideas and moving experiences from every-day people. I have been in the moving industry for 22 years and I was surprised at all the new ideas I learned from your book!"

—FRED WALLACE, PRESIDENT, ONE BIG MAN & ONE BIG TRUCK MOVING COMPANY

"A good resource book for do-it-yourself movers to learn some of the best tips in making a move easier."

—JOANNE FRIED, U-HAUL INTERNATIONAL, INC.

HOW TO SURVIVE YOUR MARRIAGE

"I love this book!"
—DONNA BRITT, HOST, LIFETIME RADIO

"Reader-friendly and packed full of good advice. They should hand this out at the marriage license counter!"
—BOB NACHSHIN, CELEBRITY DIVORCE ATTORNEY AND CO-AUTHOR OF I DO, YOU DO . . . BUT JUST SIGN HERE

"Full of honest advice from newlyweds and longtime couples. This book answers the question—'How do other people do it?'"
—ELLEN SABIN, M.P.H., M.P.A., EXECUTIVE DIRECTOR, EQUALITY IN MARRIAGE INSTITUTE

HOW TO SURVIVE YOUR BABY'S FIRST YEAR

"What to read when you're reading the other baby books. The perfect companion for your first-year baby experience."
—SUSAN REINGOLD, M.A., EDUCATOR

"*How to Survive Your Baby's First Year*…offers tried-and-true methods of baby care and plenty of insight to the most fretted about parenting topics…"
—BOOKVIEWS

"Full of real-life ideas and tips. If you love superb resource books for being the best parent you can be, you'll love *How to Survive Your Baby's First Year.*"
—ERIN BRWON CONROY, M.A.
AUTHOR, COLUMNIST, MOTHER OF TWELVE, AND CREATOR OF TOTALLYFITMOM.COM

"The Hundreds of Heads folks have done it again! Literally hundreds of moms and dads from all over offer their nuggets of wisdom—some sweet, some funny, all smart—on giving birth, coming home and bringing up baby."
—ANDREA SARVADY
AUTHOR OF BABY GAMI

Where to Seat Aunt Edna

WARNING:

This guide contains differing opinions. Hundreds of heads will not always agree. Advice taken in combination may cause unwanted side effects. Use your head when selecting advice.

Where to Seat

to Seat

Aunt

and 500

Edna

Other Great

Wedding Tips

HARRIETTE ROSE KATZ AND BESHA RODELL
SPECIAL EDITORS

Hundreds of Heads Books, LLC

ATLANTA, GEORGIA

CONTENTS

Introduction

By far the most wonderful kind of celebration I can think of is a wedding. My company, Gourmet Advisory Services, has planned thousands of events: anniversaries, bar and bat mitzvahs, birthdays, graduations, and reunions; charity galas with thousands of guests: corporate events; and intimate gatherings. I've enjoyed planning them all, but my favorite has always been weddings.

What makes weddings so special? I think it's the emotion and thought put into every detail of the wedding. Every couple is different, with a unique vision of what their wedding should be. From the location and the ceremony, to the color scheme, lighting, music, and special food, their wedding should express their individuality, their heritage, and their hopes for the future. How many parties in a person's life will ever mean as much?

Of course, weddings can be the focus of conflict and stress as well as joy. The complexity of wedding plans can be daunting. Most couples are not only first-time brides and grooms, they are also first-time party planners. There are certainly many obstacles that you may encounter on the way to the altar, but by planning ahead, seeking advice from those who have been through it before, and, most of all, being kind to yourself and those around you, you can create a meaningful celebration you'll remember with delight for years to come.

HARRIETTE ROSE KATZ
PRESIDENT
GOURMET ADVISORY SERVICES

Congratulations! You're getting married! From here on, your thoughts will be focused on love, pretty dresses, and what to do with all the fabulous gifts you receive. Right? Wrong!

While your wedding should be a magical moment in your life, planning a wedding can be one of life's most stressful experiences.

Expert advice can help you handle all those details. Books, magazines, Web sites, and consultants all contribute years of experience with varied types of weddings. Yet for many people, great wedding advice and ideas came from their own family and friends who have survived their own weddings. So we asked hundreds of brides and grooms to share their thoughts about what worked (and what didn't work) for them. If two heads are better than one, as the saying goes, then hundreds of them should be even better.

In this book, you'll find tons of tips about how to get through the whole experience, from choosing a venue for the wedding to settling down in your new life together. You'll get advice on how to take control of your wedding planning, and how to give up a little control when it's best for your sanity. There's a chapter on how to save money, and another on how to reduce stress. There are tips on how to avoid ending up on *America's Funniest Home Videos*, and how to make it through that all-important first kiss as a married couple.

So think of this book as hundreds of friends who want to help you have a smooth, stress-free, and fabulous wedding. Make the best of their good ideas, and learn from their mishaps. This is just the first step in a long and happy journey.

Besha Rodell

Let the Plans Begin: What Kind of Wedding, Where & When?

T ype "wedding stress" into Google, and you'll get over four million results. Clearly, planning a wedding is not easy. Along with engaging in everyday life (i.e., your job), you must also manage a project of hundreds of equally essential details. And it's not just any project—most couples anticipate their wedding day to be the best day of their lives. Read on: There are plenty of ideas out there to help you make the right choices.

I HAVE BEEN THROUGH university exams, relationship breakups, a mountain of school debt, and serious surgery. But nothing was as stressful as planning for my wedding.

—ANONYMOUS
TORONTO, ONTARIO, CANADA
NUMBER OF WEDDING GUESTS: 145

GO TO VEGAS! I HAD ELVIS PERFORM MY CEREMONY AT A NEON CHAPEL.

—ALEAH CLINE
SAN FRANCISCO, CALIFORNIA

FROM THE EXPERT: TREND SPOTTING

I have noticed that many couples are deciding to having a small, very private, wedding, followed by a fabulous party on a later date, even as late as after the honeymoon. It's a great way to marry with seriousness *and* celebrate with fun and energy.

The wedding date should mean something. You are going to be celebrating this date for the rest of your life.

—*TONY COLAGUORI*
PITTSBURGH,
PENNSYLVANIA
NUMBER OF WED-
DING GUESTS: 110

WE DECIDED TO GET MARRIED in the bowling alley where we met on a Saturday night. It just seemed obvious. We got married on our weekly bowling night and then bowled afterward. Right after the "kiss the bride" part, we both grabbed our bowling balls and threw them down the lane together. I wish I could tell you we both got strikes, but that didn't happen.

—*JACKIE EDMONDS*
WILLIAMSTOWN, KENTUCKY
NUMBER OF WEDDING GUESTS: 50

• • • • • • • •

I LIVE IN MAINE AND my wedding will be in Minnesota. It's challenging to plan a wedding from so far away. I've gone home a few times and am doing a lot more than my fiancé. My mom is helping me and doing things that I don't feel I need to participate in, like which sound system to get. Even though it's crazed, it works for me because when I'm back in Minnesota, I'm completely focused on maximizing my time and planning the wedding. I have wedding momentum; I'm able to accomplish a lot. Then, I go back to Maine and can take a few weeks off from it all.

—*AMY JEFFERY*
BRIDGTON, MAINE
NUMBER OF WEDDING GUESTS: 100

FOLLOW YOUR HEART: When my husband and I got married, we decided to elope instead of having a church wedding. We didn't know a lot of people, certainly not enough to fill a church, which I thought was important at the time. Plus, there were some family things going on. So we kept it simple: just the two of us. It worked out just fine, and we're still married more than 35 years later!

—*MARY BRIGHT*
ALLENTOWN, PENNSYLVANIA

"I don't care how good you are at being a social butterfly; if you want to be able to spend time with the guests at the wedding, go small—maybe up to 70 people or so."

—*SHANNON*
SAN RAFAEL, CALIFORNIA

BELIEVE IT OR NOT, I ended up getting married on April Fool's Day. We actually had planned this big wedding without even realizing the implications of the date. It wasn't until months later that someone pointed out that it was April Fool's Day. We *felt* like fools, but it was too late to change it. Luckily it didn't doom our marriage.

—*CHUCK MANION*
BETHEL PARK, PENNSYLVANIA

THE BEST WEDDINGS I've been to have been in people's backyards. One friend of mine didn't have a bar or any beer; he just got 50 bottles of champagne and a couple of pounds of strawberries, dumped them all in a big bowl with a ladle, and that's what we had to drink. Everyone was so happy at that wedding—so bubbly! How could you not be with champagne and strawberries?

—*J.G.*
CHAPEL HILL, NORTH CAROLINA
NUMBER OF WEDDING GUESTS: 85

My husband is the child of Mexican immigrants and I'm the child of hippies. We found a happy medium by having a barbecue outside with salsa dancing!

—*STACY E. MORALES*
CADIZ, KENTUCKY
NUMBER OF WEDDING GUESTS: 100

• • • • • • • •

IT'S A GOOD IDEA TO PICK a late fall or early winter date because so few people get married that time of year. Plus, you can usually bargain prices down in the winter. I'll bet we saved a couple thousand dollars by getting married in December compared to what we would have paid in June.

—*ROB MARINO*
EAST LIVERPOOL, OHIO

• • • • • • • •

IT WAS REALLY EASY to pick our date. We started by talking about what season we liked best, narrowed that down by avoiding family functions and holidays within that season, and then found a weekend that was free.

—*JOHN BAUMAN*
LYNNWOOD, WASHINGTON

• • • • • • • •

WE HAD OUR RECEPTION at a pizza parlor. It was great because it reflected our style. If you're not a fancy person and don't enjoy the type of things you see at a typical reception, like dancing and cutting the cake, don't do it. Do something you like.

—*JENNIFER*
LAS VEGAS, NEVADA
NUMBER OF WEDDING GUESTS: 4

FOREIGN AFFAIR

We got married in my hometown: Rome, Italy. I've always wanted to get married there, and since my husband likes Rome, it wasn't too hard to convince him. We invited about 120 people, but only 70 could make the trip. We would never have been able to do it all without my mother, who lives in the city where we got married. I was living 6,000 miles away in California while planning it. Fortunately, my husband and I went to Rome in December to visit venues and churches. Then, my mom booked them for us after we'd returned to the U.S. We were able to be in Rome for the three weeks leading up to the wedding and during that time got to walk through the church and do a tasting with the caterer. All of our out-of-town guests made their own travel arrangements and paid their own way and own accommodations. Two of my friends postponed their honeymoons from their July weddings, in order to attend my wedding in September.

—*M.B.*
WEEHAWKEN, NEW JERSEY
NUMBER OF WEDDING GUESTS: 70

WEATHER IS ONE BIG FACTOR that people tend to forget about. If you are going to plan a January wedding you'd better give some thought to what you'll do if there is a foot of snow. I got married in November and we had a picture-perfect day— but we had contingency plans in place. We had booked extra hotel rooms in case people couldn't get home that night, and we even bought snow shovels if we had to make a path from the limo to the church and the hall. You have to be a Boy Scout on your wedding day: be prepared for anything and everything.

—*MITZIE HAGEN*
WHEELING, WEST VIRGINIA
NUMBER OF WEDDING GUESTS: 100

WE GOT MARRIED IN OUR LIVING ROOM with our dogs. A lot of people were mad that we didn't do more; I actually lost one friend over it. Everyone wants it to be about them. I highly recommend getting married in your sweatpants, but be prepared to take a lot of crap for it.

—CHRISTINA
CHAPEL HILL, NORTH CAROLINA

• • • • • • • •

KNOW WHAT'S MOST IMPORTANT to you and participate in that part of the planning as much as you can. I wanted everything to reflect my personality. For the venue, I wanted something with an outdoor ocean view. For the band, I wanted one that was fun and lively and would get everyone dancing.

—DORI
NEW YORK, NEW YORK
NUMBER OF WEDDING GUESTS: 250

I highly recommend looking at city-owned properties, as they tend to be a lot cheaper.

—ALLAN JAFFE
PETALUMA,
CALIFORNIA
NUMBER OF WEDDING GUESTS: 90

Like many fathers before him, Steve Martin's character in *Father of the Bride* laments the high cost of, among other things, a wedding cake for his daughter's big day. That movie came out in 1991. We can only assume he would suffer greater sticker shock today. Here is the average cost of wedding components in 2005, and the percentage of increase since 1999.

	2005 Cost	% Increase
Engagement ring	$4,146	39%
Photography/videography	$2,570	103%
Ceremony/reception music	$1,250	68%
Rehearsal dinner	$1,153	51%
Flowers	$1,121	45%

BACK WHEN I GOT MARRIED, there was just no way to do it without being traditional—the church and the big, silly dress. I felt so stupid; I didn't feel at all like the princess everyone said I was supposed to feel like. If I could do it over, I'd have a blues band and get married in a field; or at the beach, where I'm really comfortable. It should be a reflection of who's getting married, not of the culture they live in.

> —AMY
> DURHAM, NORTH CAROLINA

. . . .

LOCATION IS REALLY IMPORTANT. We had a "destination" wedding—we held the ceremony in Arches National Park in Utah. My husband and I had visited that area several times and it was very special to us. We felt it would be great for our friends and family to share that place with us. It turned out wonderfully and everyone was really glad to have had the chance to go there.

> —ANONYMOUS
> ATLANTA, GEORGIA
> NUMBER OF WEDDING GUESTS: 35

. . . .

WE CONSIDERED HAVING the reception at our favorite museum, thinking it would be cheaper to rent than a hotel ballroom, but it was just the opposite! Hotels are equipped for cooking and serving food: at a museum we would have had to hire a catering company in addition to rental costs for tables, chairs, etc. We also compared the cost for a sit-down dinner and a buffet-style option: I thought the sit-down affair would be more expensive, but it was actually cheaper!

> —PATRICIA FROELICH KLIER
> WINTER PARK, FLORIDA
> NUMBER OF WEDDING GUESTS: 75

MORE THAN YOU THINK

The cost of the average wedding is $26,300. Nearly half of all couples will end up spending more than they originally budgeted.

BIG BUSINESS

In the United States, a total of $125 billion—the size of Ireland's gross domestic product—was spent on 2.1 million weddings in 2005.

GETTING HIM TO AGREE TO PICK a date was problematic. We knew we were getting married, but he was dragging his feet. One day, sitting at the table with his mother while he was in the room, I said to her, "Let's pick a date for the wedding." Once I did that, he got more serious. We picked the specific date by choosing a time frame and choosing the venue and then seeing what dates were open.

—*ANONYMOUS*
SEATTLE, WASHINGTON
NUMBER OF WEDDING GUESTS: 70

• • • • • • • •

MY HUSBAND IS A VOLUNTEER FIREMAN, so having the reception at the local fire hall was the obvious choice to me. It cost us next to nothing at all: all we had to pay for was the catering. Some members of my family felt that it looked cheap to have it at a fire hall, but really all you are talking about is a big room. If the place has a big enough dance floor and enough bathrooms, that's really all you need.

—*HELEN HUGHES*
CLEVELAND, OHIO
NUMBER OF WEDDING GUESTS: 150

The People You Love: Choosing Your Wedding Party & Inviting Guests

B y some estimates, the average wedding includes an audience of at least 150 people. It might sound like a lot, but it all leads to tough questions: How do you decide on a best man or maid of honor without offending other friends and family members? Do you have to invite Aunt Edna? Read on to learn how other couples handled these and other challenges.

THE QUESTION ALL BRIDES and grooms should ask themselves when selecting people to be in the wedding is, "Who are the people I can count on and who will be in my life ten years from now?" You need to count on these people during one of the most important days of your life.

—DORI
NEW YORK, NEW YORK
NUMBER OF WEDDING GUESTS: 250

SEVEN BRIDESMAIDS, SEVEN GROOMS. IN OUR WEDDING, IT WAS THE MORE THE MERRIER!

—MICHELE
ATLANTA, GEORGIA
NUMBER OF WEDDING GUESTS: 200

HEADLINES
Best Advice and Top Tips

- Select people for your wedding party who you think will be in your life for many years to come.

- Understand that children don't always follow the script during the ceremony—many a flower girl or ring bearer has lost his or her nerve at the last minute.

- Feel free to leave anyone off the guest list if you think he or she will cause you mental or emotional anguish—this includes parents, stepparents, siblings, etc.

- Don't have anyone in your wedding party who is cuter than you—you don't want them taking the spotlight away from you.

- If you think you'd like to invite someone, no matter how distant the relation, do it—you'll be sorry if you arrive at your big day feeling as if you left someone out.

I DECIDED TO ASK MY OLDER SISTER and her husband to be the master and mistress of the ceremony, because they're so organized and are take-charge kind of people. My fear was that my older sister would be really hurt that she wasn't standing up for me (especially since my younger sister was the maid of honor), but I explained to her that it would mean more to me to have her make sure my wedding day ran smoothly than having her stand up in front with me.

—*LESLIE*
GRAND RAPIDS, MICHIGAN

DON'T KEEP A DISTANT RELATIVE off the guest list unless you have a good reason, like money concerns. Weddings are like big family reunions; they are times when everyone from all over the place comes together. If you can afford it, there are no relatives that are too distant to invite. We had great aunts and uncles and third and fourth cousins at our wedding. It was nice to see these people, whom I had only seen when I was very young. Really it was like meeting them for the first time. And they all brought presents, too!

—*JONATHAN GRESH*
  POLAND, OHIO

FROM THE EXPERT:
WHOSE GUESTS ARE THEY, ANYWAY?

When two families come together to plan a wedding, the first issue may well be which side gets to invite the most guests?

To be fair to all sides, divide the list evenly: the bride's parents, the groom's parents, and the bridal couple each get one-third of the total. You may adjust that proportion to reflect factors such as: An older, more established bridal couple (with many friends and connections of their own, and possibly a second marriage for one or both); one side is the "hometown team" (presumably with more guests living in the area); or, simply, who's got the bigger family.

BEST OF THE BEST

I chose my dad to be my best man at my wedding. He and my mom divorced when I was young and he always lived in another city. But when I tried to think of someone else, no one came to mind. He was the guy I talked to about everything, and he loved my fiancé. When I asked him to be my best man, over the phone, there was a prolonged silence. It totally threw him; he started crying! It's one of the many great moments I remember from that time.

—J.A.
ATLANTA, GEORGIA
NUMBER OF WEDDING GUESTS: 200

CHOOSE PEOPLE WHO YOU CAN really count on to get the job done, because there's a lot more to do than just stand next to you. If you pick people only for sentimental reasons, you may add extra stress at a time when you don't need it. We had superstars who were amazing—we simply could not have done it without their help and support.

—JENNY
CARRBORO, NORTH CAROLINA

• • • • • • • •

IF YOU HAVE MORE THAN FIVE COUPLES it just gets to be too much. Limit the number of couples to no more than five standing in your wedding (not counting the best man and maid of honor). The wedding pictures, especially, suffer with that many people in them. If you have friends that you don't want to tick off by excluding them, find another role in the wedding for them. Let them seat people or help you fill out invitations. There is enough work to go around.

—STACEY YURICK
LEETONIA, OHIO
NUMBER OF WEDDING GUESTS: 125

DON'T INVITE PEOPLE if you're hoping they cannot make it. I know people who thought certain out-of-towners wouldn't make the trip, and it caused stress when those people accepted!

> —*MITCH*
> *TORONTO, ONTARIO, CANADA*
> *NUMBER OF WEDDING GUESTS: 200*

" Don't choose a ring bearer who's cuter than you. You don't want them hogging the spotlight on your wedding day. You want all the ooohhs and aaahhs for you and your wife. Every family has at least one homely little boy; he should be the ring bearer. "

> —*J.D.*
> *WATTS FLATS, NEW YORK*
> *NUMBER OF WEDDING GUESTS: 100*

I THINK WE MANAGED to miss a lot of the hassle of larger weddings by planning a simple ceremony and casual reception. Everyone at the wedding was an immediate family member or close friend, and the exclusion of some of our more far-flung relations allowed us to focus on what we really wanted the day to be.

> —*JOHN MCCARTHY*
> *TALLAHASSEE, FLORIDA*
> *NUMBER OF WEDDING GUESTS: 30*

I HAVE THREE SISTERS and couldn't decide which of them to have as my maid of honor. I didn't want to hurt anyone. I figured a slight like that could affect our relationship forever. So I had all three of them as my maids of honor. It's your wedding; you get to make the rules.

—*LISA NAGY*
BOARDMAN, OHIO
NUMBER OF WEDDING GUESTS: 100

• • • • • • • •

❝There were about 100 guests at my wedding, and I was able to interact, at least to some extent, with everyone. If there had been many more, I probably wouldn't even have remembered who was there.❞

—*GRETCHEN*
BOULDER, COLORADO
NUMBER OF WEDDING GUESTS: 100

• • • • • • • •

I HAD PEOPLE IN MY WEDDING PARTY WHO, because they were old friends and I had been in their weddings, I felt as if I had to return the favor. If I could do it over again, I'd be more selective and not worry about hurting anyone's feelings.

—*S.A.*
LAKE FOREST, CALIFORNIA
NUMBER OF WEDDING GUESTS: 150

MY FLOWER GIRL DECIDED at the last minute that she didn't want to walk down the aisle. The ring bearer walked down by himself and she stayed in the back with me until it was time for me to go. I don't think anyone even realized that she didn't walk down the aisle. It upset me at first, but then I realized that it wasn't a big deal. She was only three years old.

—*JULIE FOCKLER*
LEE'S SUMMIT, MISSOURI
NUMBER OF WEDDING GUESTS: 200

. . . .

THINK ABOUT THE PEOPLE WHO, 10 years from now, will still be your friends: not necessarily those you're interacting with on a daily basis, but those who, after going for months without talking, you can talk on the phone with and feel like you never left off. Everyone has a handful of these relationships in their lives. It's important to honor them.

—*ROBERT SALTER*
MÖNCHENGLADBACH, GERMANY
NUMBER OF WEDDING GUESTS: 100

. . . .

WE HAD A REALLY HARD TIME with the guest list, mainly because my family is so crazy. For instance, do we invite my stepfather, who is estranged from my mother? He was a big part of my childhood, and I knew he'd be offended if we didn't. But it would make a few people uncomfortable, and possibly add to our stress. In the end you have to decide if you're doing it for you or for appearances. We decided we couldn't handle the extra stress, and while it caused a bit of drama, at least I can remember my wedding as being a happy day.

—*FRED*
WASHINGTON, D.C.
NUMBER OF WEDDING GUESTS: 90

Imagine that while you are putting the guest list together you have a heart attack and die. Who shows up at the funeral? Those are the people you invite to the wedding.

—*TRACY LAVALEE*
DRY RIDGE,
KENTUCKY

I HAD AN AMAZINGLY WONDERFUL, smooth, and stress-free wedding. Why? I didn't invite my mother-in-law—she is a horror. In fact, I didn't invite any family members who agitated me. I didn't arrive at this decision by myself, of course. I talked with my fiancé about it. He agreed. My philosophy is, if they upset you, cut them out!

—PAULA
WESTPORT, CONNECTICUT
NUMBER OF WEDDING GUESTS: 11

• • • • • • • •

"Ask yourself what one person you would call if you found yourself in jail and needing bail and a ride without your parents finding out: That's the person to be your best man or maid of honor."

—VAL TOSEKI
CANFIELD, OHIO
NUMBER OF WEDDING GUESTS: 100

• • • • • • • •

IF YOU HAVE A FEELING you should invite someone, do it. If not, you'll regret it later. I didn't invite an old friend because we hadn't been in touch for a while. But he's an important person to me and my husband (and was there when my husband and I first met), and I'm mad at myself for not including him.

—D.R.
TORONTO, ONTARIO, CANADA
NUMBER OF WEDDING GUESTS: 190

BEING FROM A SMALL TOWN means inviting everyone you know, everyone your grandmother knows, and everyone *they* know. We had to find a reception site that would accommodate the number of guests, and with the food we had to keep the cost per head low. We ended up going with "heavy finger foods," and had to hire a DJ (as opposed to a live band) due to the overall expense of everything else.

> —KATIE
> DALLAS, TEXAS
> NUMBER OF WEDDING GUESTS: *400*

- - - - - - - -

I WAS GOING TO HAVE MY FRIEND Shirley as my maid of honor, but she's too good-looking. You don't want to leave any chance that the maid of honor or any of the bridesmaids could steal the show: You want to make sure you are the center of attention. You can do that by leaving the best-looking one of your friends out of the wedding. I just picked the plainest-looking ones as bridesmaids so that I was sure the spotlight would be on me.

> —DAISY NARR
> ZIRKLE, VIRGINIA
> NUMBER OF WEDDING GUESTS: *100*

- - - - - - - -

CHOOSING A BEST MAN: No matter what, you have to go with family. I have one brother, but he's 10 years older and lives in Minnesota. I see him only three or four times a year. So I went with my college roomate as my best man. We were thick as thieves at the time. Now, 14 years later, I have pretty much fallen out of touch with him. But my brother has always been my brother. That was the one decision I wish I could take back.

> —MATT TIMMONS
> CALLA, OHIO
> NUMBER OF WEDDING GUESTS: *100*

It comes down to this ridiculous question: "Who am I willing to spend $90 on?" It's the worst feeling, having to cut those last people off the list.

> —ANONYMOUS
> CHAPEL HILL,
> NORTH CAROLINA
> NUMBER OF WEDDING GUESTS: *250*

INVITE ADVICE

DID YOU KNOW THAT WEDDING INVITATIONS come unassembled? I ordered hundreds and my mom put in hours of work folding them! To help speed up the process, I organized a little luncheon—me, my mother and my husband's mother—and we all assembled the invitations together.

> —*CARA M. RAICH*
> *NEW YORK, NEW YORK*
> *NUMBER OF WEDDING GUESTS: 200*

• • • • • • • •

WHEN SENDING OUT YOUR INVITATIONS, you have to specify whether or not children are invited. Don't leave it to chance. We wanted to have all the children in the family at the wedding, so we specifically said that in the invitations.

> —*HILDE PARSONS*
> *GREEN MOUNT, VIRGINIA*
> *NUMBER OF WEDDING GUESTS: 100*

• • • • • • • •

PUT SOME DRESS GUIDELINES FOR THE WEDDING in the invitations. You wouldn't believe how many guests showed up in jeans.

> —*J.B.*
> *COVINGTON, KENTUCKY*
> *NUMBER OF WEDDING GUESTS: 100*

• • • • • • • •

HERE'S A MUST: YOU HAVE TO HANDWRITE not only the outside addresses on the wedding invitations but the return-address envelopes that go inside, too. I just got an invitation to a wedding recently that had labels on the return envelopes. I think that looks terrible. It's little things like that that are important.

> —*D.E.*
> *HARRISONBURG, VIRGINIA*
> *NUMBER OF WEDDING GUESTS: 275*

I WROTE MY WEDDING INVITATIONS BY HAND. According to Miss Manners, handwriting your cards is actually fancier then getting them printed and they obviously cost a lot less. But don't do it all in one day: spread it out!

—LISA OLKON VANDESTEEG
ST. PAUL, MINNESOTA
NUMBER OF WEDDING GUESTS: 60

• • • • • • • • •

WHEN MY HUSBAND AND I FIRST MET, we exchanged phone numbers and little notes reminding each other to please call on these little slips of paper. We didn't realize until we started planning the wedding that we had both kept them. So we had them combined and blown up on one sheet of paper and turned it into the background of the paper we had the invitations printed on. People seemed to really like the idea. It added something very personal to the invitations.

—MOLLY YACKEL
JAMESTOWN, NEW YORK
NUMBER OF WEDDING GUESTS: 150

IF YOU HAVE MORE THAN ONE BROTHER, like me, and don't want to hurt the feelings of one by choosing the other as best man, then you have to compromise. I asked my brother Keith to be my best man, but then I told my brother John that he would be the godfather of our first-born. That seemed to satisfy both of them.

—TIM SCHADE
UNITY, OHIO
NUMBER OF WEDDING GUESTS: 200

• • • • • • • • •

MY FATHER-IN-LAW IS INDIAN, and it was important to him to invite many members of the community to our wedding. To me, a wedding is intimate, and I was uncomfortable with the thought of looking out at an audience of close to 500 people (most of whom were strangers to me) on my day! The way we solved the problem was to have a 400-person, Indian-style reception the following week. It was important for us to honor my husband's dad's culture and to respect his wishes. It worked out great; we found a balance that made everybody happy.

—JENIFER MANN
CASTRO VALLEY, CALIFORNIA
NUMBER OF WEDDING GUESTS: 35

• • • • • • • •

YES, U

When writing invitations, traditional British spelling is often used for the words "honour" and "favour."

I CHOSE NOT TO INVITE my biological father because he didn't raise me, and my mother hates him and hasn't spoken to him in 40 years. The problem was, I couldn't leave him out and invite my half-brother, whom I dearly love. I decided to be completely honest: I told my half-brother why I wasn't going to invite him, and I said that there will be lots of other special occasions for us to make memories together. He understood.

—PAULA
WESTPORT, CONNECTICUT
NUMBER OF WEDDING GUESTS: 11

FROM THE EXPERT:
ON THE MARCH

How many people should be in the wedding party? My advice is this: If you love them, don't leave them out of your wedding party. You will regret it if you do. It's far better to have an army standing up with you than to risk harming a relationship.

At a recent wedding, we had 45 people in the wedding party: that was immense! We had 11 bridesmaids and 11 groomsmen; a matron of honor and a maid of honor; two best men; numerous flower girls and six ring bearers; grandparents and parents. It was magnificent, but it was long. A processional like that can take half an hour. If your wedding party has grown into a crowd, you may want to ask the officiant to try to make the ceremony shorter. Most will accommodate your request.

ERR ON THE SIDE OF BEING GENEROUS and inclusive. I read a wedding book by Miss Manners: Her basic philosophy was to *first* figure out who needed to be included, and *then* decide what kind of event could accommodate them. If you have a ton of people, you'll need a less fancy event. If you have a bunch of best friends, that means you'll have a lot of bridesmaids.

—*ANONYMOUS*
WASHINGTON, D.C.
NUMBER OF WEDDING GUESTS: 150

FROM THE EXPERT:
ENGAGEMENT PARTIES

Some engagement parties can be early celebrations for everyone. But many serve as a way to introduce the couple's families to one another.

If the bride's family gives the party, the mother might invite family friends who have known the bride growing up; aunts, uncles, and other relatives of the mother's generation and older; and the groom's family in the same generation, as well as the groom.

A party like this is almost always a cocktail party, and sometimes given at home. It's always a lovely, endearing occasion.

Details!
The Reception,
the Cake,
the Music
& More

D*id you hear the one about the bride who forgot to order her own wedding cake? We wish it were just a joke. But alas, things—even important things—slip through the cracks during the planning of a wedding. Read on for tips on how to pick the right vendors, how to avoid catastrophe when your vendors don't come through, and some inspiring stories of people who have handled these important details by themselves—and survived.*

IF YOU DO YOUR RESEARCH and choose a vendor— whether florists, musicians, or photographers— micromanaging them will probably not get you what you want. Tell them your ideas, and then listen to what they have to say.

—*RINA F.*
GREAT NECK, NEW YORK

THIS IS THE BIGGEST PARTY YOU WILL EVER THROW. MAKE IT GOOD!

—*STEVE J.*
SAN DIEGO, CALIFORNIA
NUMBER OF WEDDING GUESTS: 175

HEAD LINES
Best Advice and Top Tips

■ Make a list of important photos you want taken and give it to your photographer in advance.

■ Be sure to taste all the food and cake that will be served at your wedding in advance.

■ If you hire a live band, be sure you hear them play *before* your wedding day.

■ Consider silk flowers instead of real ones—they hold up much better over time.

■ Your reception is the most important party you will ever throw—splurge wherever you can.

WHEN WE GOT MARRIED, my mother-in-law was just opening her flower store. She was *very* interested in being involved in all wedding preparations. I figured that she knew flowers and I didn't have very strong opinions about them, so why not give it all to her? Before the ceremony, when the photographer was getting us ready, the flowers were late. The photographer was hysterical and finally grabbed some flowers from a nearby vase, so some of my photos have the stand-in flowers. They looked pretty good; to me, they seemed pretty close to the real bouquet. My advice: Let it go; it will be just fine.

—*ANONYMOUS*
WASHINGTON, D.C.
NUMBER OF WEDDING GUESTS: 150

FROM THE EXPERT: GLOWING DÉCOR

Candles make everything look sparkly and fabulous. I order an abundance of votive candles to be placed at tables to accent the centerpieces, at table settings, and around the perimeter of the room. Everywhere. Candles give the room a romantic glow.

LOOK AT THE RECEPTION as the biggest and most important party you'll ever throw in your life. Even if you are thrifty, this is one time in your life when you have to go all out. Don't be cheap with the reception venue. Have it somewhere super-nice; somewhere you couldn't ordinarily even afford to walk into. We had ours in a four-star hotel in downtown Pittsburgh; it was totally awesome. I had never even ventured into the place before. It turned out to be all I could have hoped for, and more.

> —*EILEEN*
> *PITTSBURGH, PENNSYLVANIA*

· · · · · · · ·

THE WEDDING RECEPTION is not the time to experiment. Stick with the basics. Everyone likes chicken. Everyone likes spaghetti. Everyone likes potatos and green beans. If you or your caterer has a new Chinese dish that he has been dying to try out on a large crowd tell him to try it on someone else. We had all those basics along with all the bread and butter you could eat, and I didn't hear any complaining. Everybody likes bread.

> —*MIKE POUND*
> *UNITY, OHIO*
> *NUMBER OF WEDDING GUESTS: 200*

SAY IT WITH FLOWERS

During the Victorian era, the popularity of a book called *The Language of Flowers* inspired women to compose bouquets with special meanings—each flower having its own significance. As an example, ivy stands for fidelity, violets for modesty and hope. Jasmine stands for happiness, while ranunculus means the recipient is radiant with charm.

Today's bride chooses her wedding bouquet based more on considerations of style—and the possibilities are endless. Here are some suggestions to make the process simpler:

- If cost is a concern, select flowers that are in season.
- Ask your florist to recommend flowers that are sturdy enough to look fresh all day.
- Give your florist a visual. Don't just tell him or her that your color is purple; bring a sample of fabric showing the specific shade.
- Look for pictures of bouquets you like and bring them to your florist for ideas.
- Don't let your bouquet make more of a statement than you do! The bouquet should complement, not overwhelm, you and your ensemble.
- Consider silk flowers—they are economical, the time of year is not a concern, and you will be able to display your bouquet at home long after the wedding.
- Do some research: Look into the meaning of specific flowers and create a bouquet that says just what you want it to.

BE SURE TO SAMPLE IN ADVANCE at least a bite of the same type of cake that will be served at your wedding. Just because a cake looks nice doesn't mean it will taste good. Ours was awful. We could see people digging in and then putting it aside.

—*BRETT DAVID*
HARRISONBURG, VIRGINIA

" People judge your wedding by the food at your reception. We wanted to make sure our meal was one guests truly enjoyed, so we had it catered by a quality place. "

—*ROBERT SALTER*
MÖNCHENGLADBACH, GERMANY
NUMBER OF WEDDING GUESTS: 100

IN ADDITION TO A PROFESSIONAL photographer, make sure you hire someone to take a video of the wedding. You get all kinds of stuff that still pictures can't give you. Years later, it will give your kids a chance to laugh at how young and goofy you look. For me, another bonus was that the video is the last one that my father appears on before he died. We play it from time to time just to see him.

—*ANDREA WEIGAND*
WOODWORTH, OHIO

I'M HAPPY TO SHARE MY NUMBER ONE piece of advice on choosing flowers: *Do not plan your wedding to be the same weekend as Mother's Day.* Unfortunately, that's what I did! And I found out that 99 percent of florists don't even *take on* weddings that weekend, as it's their second busiest time of the year (behind Valentine's Day).

—*K.R.*
TAMPA, FLORIDA
NUMBER OF WEDDING GUESTS: 115

LOOK AT US!

Today, four in ten couples have a wedding Web page.

DON'T THINK YOU HAVE TO HAVE a big white cake just because it's traditional. My wife and I are chocoholics, and we figured since it's our wedding, let them eat chocolate cake with chocolate frosting. Ours was a three-tiered, chocolate-goo-layered extravaganza. Years later, we *still* get comments from people about what a great cake that was.

—*MATT*
SAN CARLOS, CALIFORNIA

HAVE SOMEONE YOU TRUST—a parent or older relative—go over the song list. Since I was one of the first of my friends to get married, I really wanted my college friends to have a good time at our reception, so I chose songs I knew young people would dance to. I neglected to consider the older relatives and friends who would loathe such music. In fact, I am embarrassed to admit that one or two songs on my list were inappropriate, better suited to a club atmosphere than a wedding. What can I say? I was young and stupid.

—*M.H.*
RICHMOND, INDIANA
NUMBER OF WEDDING GUESTS: 265

I FOUND A GREAT IDEA FOR TABLE SETTINGS. We got married in the fall, and we went out and found fall leaves that were mostly flat and intact. Then we used them to mark each table setting with a small welcoming message to our guests. It really gave a spark of originality to our reception.

> —DENISE JUNKER
> INDEPENDENCE, KENTUCKY
> NUMBER OF WEDDING GUESTS: 200

. . . .

WE HAD AN ULTRA-MINI-MICRO WEDDING on the beach in Hawaii. The only flower we had was an orchid we found on the grass while walking to the beach. Lilia put it in her hair. Oh, and we were each wearing orchid leis, but we didn't pick them out: the wedding coordinator provided them.

> —T.B.
> ATLANTA, GEORGIA
> NUMBER OF WEDDING GUESTS: 0

. . . .

IT'S ESSENTIAL TO HIRE a wedding consultant. Our wedding consultant was great—she saved me hours of time because she researched everything and presented me with options. It would have taken me weeks to do what she did in hours.

> —ANONYMOUS
> ATLANTA, GEORGIA
> NUMBER OF WEDDING GUESTS: 75

. . . .

WHEN FIGURING OUT HOW LARGE a wedding cake you will need, don't forget that you will not be serving the top tier of the cake to your guests: You always save that to have with your wife on your first anniversary.

> —MICHAEL CONWAY
> HARRISONBURG, VIRGINIA
> NUMBER OF WEDDING GUESTS: 250

BREAKING DOWN THE NUMBERS

Approximately 50 percent of your wedding budget will go to the reception. Flowers, photography, music and attire will each take 10 percent.

WHEN CHOOSING YOUR FLOWERS, I recommend that you buy silk ones instead of fresh flowers. It's true that silk costs more and fresh flowers smell nicer, but with silk ones you can keep them forever. It's a very nice keepsake to have. I pull them out once in a while, and nothing takes me back to the ceremony like looking at my bouquet.

—*R.D.*
KEEZLETOWN, VIRGINIA
NUMBER OF WEDDING GUESTS: 200

• • • • • • • •

I PLANNED MY WEDDING from another city while I was working full-time, so I hired a coordinator. Still, some things fell through the cracks. I came back home a few days before the wedding and my mother asked me about the cake: I forgot to order one! I raced over to a bakery and asked if a wedding cake could be ready for my wedding on October 13. The owner answered, "Sure—a year is plenty of time!" She didn't realize that I meant the October 13 that was four days away! A rush cake was ordered; it all worked out in the end. Phew!

—*CARA M. RAICH*
NEW YORK, NEW YORK
NUMBER OF WEDDING GUESTS: 200

• • • • • • • •

IF MONEY IS A CONCERN, you might want to go with a DJ instead of hiring a band. We found that a band's fee is usually based on a four-hour minimum. Expect to pay from $3,500 to $5,500. But we only paid $1,500 for our DJ and he agreed to do an hour after he was supposed to quit for only $100. I think he was having as good a time as everybody else. The bottom line is to get people dancing. And they will dance to good music whether it comes from a live band or a CD.

—*A.G.*
HUBBARD, OHIO
NUMBER OF WEDDING GUESTS: 100

FROM THE EXPERT: KEY TO SUCCESS #1 —GOOD MUSIC

Remember, the wedding reception is basically a big party. Like other kinds of parties, it depends on some basic factors for success. Great music is the first key to success.

I've seen it happen at weddings. The same crowd, the same food, same location, same service: when the music was great, the party was great; when the music was lousy, the party was lousy.

Make sure the music at your reception—DJ or live, swing or hip-hop—is the best you can find. Take the time to audition different groups, and don't settle.

Music makes the party.

MINIMAL BUT HIGH-QUALITY DÉCOR IS FINE. We had sparse flowers and table settings, and it looked very lovely, in a tranquil way.

> —JEN
> SAN CARLOS, CALIFORNIA

• • • • • • • • •

MAKE SURE YOU GET to see a full video—and not just "best of" clips—when you choose your video guy.

> —M.B.
> SAN FRANCISCO, CALIFORNIA
> NUMBER OF WEDDING GUESTS: 110

FROM THE EXPERT: KEY TO SUCCESS #2 —A GOOD CROWD

It seems obvious that to have a good reception you need guests who like to have good time. It's too late to order up a new set of party-ready friends and relatives, but you can give some thought to what kind of reception is most likely to bring out the best in your group. Perhaps you need a quiet corner where your hard-of-hear-ing, elderly relatives will be able to converse, or some space for the lit-tle kids to run around, or a dance floor big enough for your friends to really cut loose. You may also want to supply ear plugs for your elderly guests.

Most important, do what you can to make sure your reception feels welcoming, relaxing, and celebratory for everyone. When your guests are having a great time, you will, too.

WE ASKED LOTS OF GUESTS to take videos, and supply us with the raw footage. Then we asked our friend who is a video edi-tor to make us a tape instead of getting us a gift. It was the best gift he could've given us! It was all so much more personal; the people taking the videos knew the guests and us, and we have the best wedding video I've ever seen.

—K.B.
SAN FRANCISCO, CALIFORNIA

THINGS TO DO

6 MONTHS BEFORE YOUR WEDDING

____Mail save-the-date announcements letting guests know the date, time, and location of the wedding.

____Purchase your favors, if you're not making them.

____Start thinking about your rehearsal dinner and make a guest list.

____Register for wedding gifts.

____Order your wedding cake.

____Reserve your transportation to and from the wedding and reception.

____Order stationery.

____Select clothing for groom and groomsmen.

____Buy your wedding rings.

____Book wedding night accommodations for you and your out-of-town guests.

____Buy gifts for your wedding party, your parents, and each other.

3 MONTHS BEFORE YOUR WEDDING

____Make a list of important pictures you'd like your wedding photographer to take.

____Go over the menu with your caterer.

____Discuss the details of the service with your officiant.

____If you intend to write your own vows, begin them.

____Mail your wedding invitations.

____Plan your hair and makeup. Book your stylist, if you're using one, and have him or her experiment with different looks.

____Schedule your wedding rehearsal and rehearsal dinner.

____Make appointments for the blood test and marriage license.

IN MY EXPERIENCE, many wedding coordinators are not warm and friendly. They order people around and the wedding party just rolls their eyes!

—ANONYMOUS
TORONTO, ONTARIO, CANADA
NUMBER OF WEDDING GUESTS: 175

● ● ● ● ● ● ● ●

" Put disposable cameras on each of the tables so that your guests can take pictures for you. It doesn't cost much, and you will have lots of shots that you'd never get otherwise. "

—DEBBIE PRZYWARTY
IRWIN, PENNSYLVANIA
NUMBER OF WEDDING GUESTS: 100

● ● ● ● ● ● ● ●

THE MOST IMPORTANT THING about the cake is how it looks. I can't even remember what flavor my own wedding cake was. Believe me, nobody will remember how it tasted, but you'll have the pictures for life!

—A.J.
SAN FRANCISCO, CALIFORNIA
NUMBER OF WEDDING GUESTS: 135

STAR BRIGHT

Want some inspiration for your bridal bouquet? Look to the stars—celebrities, that is. Here's what some famous brides chose to carry as they walked down the aisle:

- Miami Heat star Shaquille O'Neal and bride Shaunie Nelson selected purple roses for their wedding—purple being the color of royalty.

- When she married Brad Pitt, Jennifer Aniston carried a bouquet of pale Dutch Vendela roses accented with sprigs of green hydrangea.

- *Law & Order: SVU* star Mariska Hargitay chose ivory roses and fragrant gardenias mixed with lily-of-the-valley accents when she married fellow actor Peter Hermann.

- When *All My Children* stars Alexa Havins and Justin Bruening wed, the bride had tiny princess-cut diamonds embedded into the petals of her bouquet of white orchids.

- Britney Spears opted for a little extra sparkle as well: the handle of her white-rose bouquet was tipped with Swarovski crystals.

- Jennifer Lopez chose white stephanotis blossoms mixed into a pure-white bouquet of orchids and roses.

- TV star Debra Messing carried a bouquet of elegant, long-stemmed calla lilies at her wedding.

- Perhaps the most famous "other woman" of all time, Camilla Parker-Bowles, selected a bouquet of yellow, purple, and white primroses with lily of the valley when she wed Prince Charles.

- When Melania Knauss married Donald Trump, she chose to forgo the bouquet altogether, and walked down the aisle carrying a family rosary instead.

I'VE ATTENDED WEDDINGS THAT SEEMED as though the event were being held for the photographer! Many of the photos were so time-consuming and staged. A professional photographer friend offered to take our pictures as a wedding present. While we did have some posed photographs that we cherish, our friend took more of a photojournalistic approach, documenting things as they occurred, rather than posing them. She included photographs of the setting and the food, and lots of fun, candid shots that really captured the mood of the day.

—*CAROL*
EASTON, PENNSYLVANIA

• • • • • • • •

MAKE A LIST OF PICTURES you want taken by the photographer. My sister-in-law took our pictures, which came out fine, but the majority of them were of my new family and not a lot of my own family. I don't have any pictures of some of the guests.

—*ALEXANDRA*
NORWALK, CONNECTICUT

• • • • • • • •

INSTEAD OF BUYING a wedding photo package, just pay for the photographer's time and photo DVD. I know people who spent up to $2,400 on their wedding photos. For just $275, we paid the photographer for his time and a DVD of all of the photos—hundreds of them. Now we can have pictures printed anywhere, such as CVS or Target photo centers, and we'll pay the photographer to make prints of the most special photos. More and more photographers offer this option now.

—*TINA COUCH*
FRISCO, TEXAS
NUMBER OF WEDDING GUESTS: 51

MAKE SURE YOU WILL OWN the negatives of your wedding pictures. Many photographers keep them; it's a way for them to make more money when you order more prints. But we found a great photographer who let us own the negatives. We were able to get prints of shots we liked at a much cheaper rate and then put together small albums for family members for the first Hanukkah and Christmas after our wedding.

> —DAVID HUBBELL
> KIRKLAND, WASHINGTON
> NUMBER OF WEDDING GUESTS: 110

Choose your cake based on taste, not looks.

> —JOHN
> ATHENS, GEORGIA
> NUMBER OF WEDDING GUESTS: 200

. . . .

HAVE SOME FUN WITH your cake toppers. Instead of the little bride and groom all dressed up in tux and gown, we had these two little figurines that we felt represented us in our normal life—a guy fishing and a girl sunbathing. Our guests cracked up.

> —ELLIS
> SEATTLE, WASHINGTON

. . . .

WHEN HIRING A PHOTOGRAPHER, keep in mind the type of photos you want. Do you want candid shots? When you're reviewing a photographer's work, look from the beginning to the end of the wedding day to see what images were captured. Do they evoke a feeling of what that person is thinking? Do you want to see a lot of detail in shots? Look for shots of the bride's flowers and dress. Put those special shots you must have in writing in the photographer's contract. Give the photographer a strict timeline for these shots and then assign a wedding guest to watch the clock!

> —ANONYMOUS
> LONG VALLEY, NEW JERSEY

WHEN I FOUND MYSELF FORCED to dance in a ridiculous conga line early on in the reception, I knew our DJ had paid no attention to my requested songs and type of music.

—*ERIN DARWIN*
SAN FRANCISCO, CALIFORNIA

• • • • • • • • •

WE FLEW IN A FAMILY FRIEND who is a photographer for the week of the wedding. We supplied him with the film and he took photos the entire week. That way we did not have to worry about capturing the moments; we were able to just live each moment fully.

—*LACEY YANTIS BLANK*
BOTHELL, WASHINGTON
NUMBER OF WEDDING GUESTS: 120

Fashion Sense: The Dress, the Tuxedo & Other Style Points

*A*nd then there's the bride's wedding dress, the bridesmaids' dresses, and the tuxedos for the groom and his groomsmen. You want to make the perfect choice. After all, what you and your wedding party wear on your wedding day will stay with you for the rest of your life—in pictures, video, and memory. So where do you start? Read on for answers.

START SHOPPING EARLY. As soon as I got engaged I started compiling a list of what I needed. Then I started watching sales. I traveled to Oregon to buy my wedding dress: There is no sales tax there, so it was worth the two-hour drive. I saved hundreds of dollars on my gown, shoes, and accessories.

—*MELISSA*
TACOMA, WASHINGTON
NUMBER OF WEDDING GUESTS: 110

WAIT FOR THE SALES! I FOUND A DRESS FOR $200 (REGULAR PRICE $800)!

—*PAMELA*
CHICAGO, ILLINOIS
NUMBER OF WEDDING GUESTS: 100

HEAD LINES
Best Advice and Top Tips

- When picking your wedding shoes, remember that you'll have to wear them all day long.

- Don't let the groom-to-be go to the tuxedo shop on his own, or you risk being unpleasantly surprised by his selection.

- Consider the body types of all your bridesmaids when selecting a dress style.

- Make a list of the clothing and accessories you will need for your wedding as soon as possible—that way you have time to watch for sales.

- If you are doing your own hair and makeup for the wedding, be sure you experiment before the big day.

IF YOU ARE A GOOD SEAMSTRESS, make your own dress: It is cheaper, it has more meaning and you are guaranteed that not many brides will have that same dress, nor will you find it in a magazine! I picked out a simple pattern—a long dress with an empire waist with a hooded cape edged in white lace. I remember staying home from work and sewing from morning till night to get it done. People insist on spending hundreds, sometimes thousands of dollars on a dress worn for less than nine hours. I felt pretty and content wearing mine, knowing that it cost maybe $30 at the time. It is the fondest memory of my wedding day.

—B.L.
CHICAGO, ILLINOIS
NUMBER OF WEDDING GUESTS: 25

IF YOU DECIDE TO DO THE "something borrowed, something blue" thing, make sure at least one of those items is from your mom: It means so much more. For my wedding I borrowed a handkerchief from my mother: It was the same one her mother had given her for her wedding. And I plan to lend it to my own daughter for her wedding.

—*KELLEY FREID*
POLAND, OHIO
NUMBER OF WEDDING GUESTS: 150

• • • • • • • •

MY WEDDING WAS IN THE DAYTIME, so I chose ivory dinner jackets, because you're not supposed to wear black jackets before dinnertime, and because my granddaddy had an ivory dinner jacket. I also selected boutonnieres that were purple/red thistle blossom and clover blossom, not because I'm Scottish but because I grew up on a farm and those are weeds. They were a bit prickly for hugs, but pretty cool.

—*JOHN*
ATHENS, GEORGIA
NUMBER OF WEDDING GUESTS: 200

• • • • • • • •

FOR THE CEREMONY, THE WEDDING DRESS should be very beautiful. For the reception, everyone should have a really hot Barbie-style dress, a dance-party wedding dress that can be totally flirty and fun. My Barbie dress was short, sleeveless, vanilla silk, with a lot of white Cinderella bows and ribbons. I wore it with my mother's white go-go boots. It was a thousand times more fun to dance in than the dress from the ceremony would have been. And when a bride tries to rock out in a big wedding dress, she looks like a big white Christmas tree trying to shake it!

—*KAMI*
CAPE COD, MASSACHUSETTS
NUMBER OF WEDDING GUESTS: 150

Those bridal trade shows are an awesome way to get free cake.

—*JIM*
RALEIGH,
NORTH CAROLINA

HANG THE COST!

Average price of wedding dresses featured in the special wedding spread of *The New York Times* magazine: $5,153.57.

NEVER LET YOUR HUSBAND PICK OUT his own tuxedo. My fiancé was talked into a really trendy, over-the-top, gray number that would have been just horrid. I wanted to be surprised, but luckily, he asked my sister to give him a second opinion. Crisis averted.

—*D.E.*
SAN FRANCISCO, CALIFORNIA
NUMBER OF WEDDING GUESTS: 200

• • • • • • • •

WHEN PICKING OUT YOUR WEDDING SHOES, consider more than just how they look. Remember, you are going to be wearing these shoes for a while. I chose a heel that was a little too thin and a little too high. It made walking down the aisle a little trickier than it should have been.

—*ALICE DUKE*
COVINGTON, KENTUCKY

• • • • • • • •

MY MOTHER-IN-LAW AND I made my wedding dress together. We were both into sewing, and it was a wonderful way for us to bond. Since it wasn't a first marriage for me, we made it out of this amazing scarlet-and-silver silk. I had a red MGB at the time, and I made the dress to match the car. It sounds silly, I know, but it did look pretty cool, driving up in that red car in that red dress.

—*SUSANNA*
CHARLESTON, WEST VIRGINIA

• • • • • • • •

I WENT DRESS SHOPPING IN New York City with my three best friends and we found my dress in the first store we went into. I still tried on 10 others just to be sure, but I eventually went back to that one. It was pretty expensive—$800!

—*M.B.*
WEEHAWKEN, NEW JERSEY
NUMBER OF WEDDING GUESTS: 70

I DON'T RECOMMEND THAT the bride do her own hair. But if you want to do it yourself, and you are going to try something you've never done before, experiment before the big day. I thought it would be a nice personal touch to do my own hair. But it turned out to be an unmitigated disaster. I ended up running to a salon at the last minute and begging them to take me. Let a professional do it.

—*PAM WAXTER*
KEEZLETOWN, VIRGINIA
NUMBER OF WEDDING GUESTS: 175

LET THE BRIDE CHOOSE YOUR TUXEDO. She has strong opinions; most men only have limits and aversions. Take her to the store, work up an arbitrary but strong opinion, and then let her choose what she wants you to wear. When she picks out the first tux, dislike it; this is a test. On the second or third tux, start out noncommittal, examine it slowly and then express a very positive opinion.

—*EVAN*
ATLANTA, GEORGIA
NUMBER OF WEDDING GUESTS: 110

JUST AS THE BRIDE IS SUPPOSED to be the center of attention at her wedding, the groom is supposed to be the perfect gentleman. You're wearing a tux, after all. Most guys getting married in the modern world don't have a clue what that means. I recommend picking up an etiquette book; there are a million of them. You don't have to follow it word for word, but it will certainly make you feel more comfortable in a tux. Also, ask your dad for any advice on how to act; he'll be honored to help you.

—*J.A.*
ATLANTA, GEORGIA
NUMBER OF WEDDING GUESTS: 200

With makeup, less is more!! I went so over the top with the makeup and hair that I cringe at all of my photos.

—*ALEAH CLINE*
SAN FRANCISCO,
CALIFORNIA

BRIDESMAIDS DRESSES

PICK OUT THE DRESS YOU WANT the bridesmaids to wear *before* you take those girls anywhere near a bridal store. If you want to take the maid of honor with you for another opinion, that's fine. But don't take all six of those girls in there while you are trying to pick out a dress. If you do, you'll get what I got—six different girls wanting six different dresses. And then how do you settle that dispute without upsetting somebody?

> —*P.B.*
> *CANFIELD, OHIO*
> *NUMBER OF WEDDING GUESTS: 175*

• • • • • • • •

THE SAME EVENING THAT MY HUSBAND-TO-BE told me how many bridesmaids I could have (three, because he had three friends he wanted as groomsmen), he also said, "And you can have any color you want, except blue." Well, blue is my favorite color and I'm pretty independent. All of my bridesmaids wore blue. He can't say he didn't know what he was getting! Go with what you love, no matter what!

> —*SUSAN*
> *TAYLOR, TEXAS*
> *NUMBER OF WEDDING GUESTS: 130*

• • • • • • • •

I HAD EIGHT PEOPLE TO OUTFIT FOR THE WEDDING, and they represented the biggest variety of figures possible. I started out looking for a dress that would look OK on all of them, then quickly realized that my sister at 100 pounds and my friend at 200 pounds were going to look ridiculous in the same dress. And I had never seen my friend Pixie in a dress at all. I finally told them to find something in black velvet of any length, in any style. They came in a variety of dresses, and Pixie wore a pants suit. Everyone looked fabulous: They would have all looked really stupid in the same dark purple dress, which is where I was going at first.

> —*ANONYMOUS*
> *WASHINGTON, D.C.*
> *NUMBER OF WEDDING GUESTS: 150*

I LEARNED THE HARD WAY THAT YOU SHOULD stay away from sleeveless and anything off the shoulder. I had never really seen some of my friends' arms and shoulders before and I realized they were better off under cover. Unless you know that all your bridesmaids are OK in that department, I say play it safe and cover 'em up.

—*M.J.*
FRANKFORT, KENTUCKY

• • • • • • • •

DON'T WORRY ABOUT BUYING MATCHING OUTFITS for the bridesmaids. Instead, find stuff that they can wear again. You'll have happier bridesmaids this way! I had a size 2 bridesmaid, a size 22 bridesmaid, and a 10-year-old junior bridesmaid. I went to a department store, and within 30 minutes the sales associate had found three dresses—one purple, one blue and one a gray-green.

—*LISA OLKON VANDESTEEG*
ST. PAUL, MINNESOTA
NUMBER OF WEDDING GUESTS: 60

• • • • • • • •

DON'T SET YOUR MIND ON ONE PARTICULAR STYLE of bridesmaid dress. Be open to other patterns, fabrics and designs. I had something so specific in mind that, after five months of looking, I still couldn't find it. Because I hadn't even con- sidered a Plan B, my mom was forced to find whatever she could during a last-minute scramble. Unfortunately, the dresses she chose were hideous. I hated them!

—*KAREN HUGHES*
DENVER, COLORADO
NUMBER OF WEDDING GUESTS: 200

I RECOMMEND GOING SIMPLE when picking out a tux. I found mine in about 30 minutes. It's hard to go wrong with a classic black tuxedo: when you Look back at the event, you won't find yourself wondering why you decided to go with the frilly, multihued cummerbund.

—*JOHN MCCARTHY*
TALLAHASSEE, FLORIDA
NUMBER OF WEDDING GUESTS: 30

· · · · · · · ·

" I had the oldest, crappiest tuxedo ever. But you know what? It was black, it fit, and it looks just fine in the photos. If anybody noticed, they never said anything. I'm not sure it's that important. "

—*PAUL*
MINNEAPOLIS, MINNESOTA

· · · · · · · ·

EVERY GROOM GETS HIS HAIR CUT before the wedding. Most guys probably do what I did, which is to get it cut the morning of the wedding. But you should do it a week or 10 days ahead so that the hair has a chance to settle. Looking at my wedding photos, it's obvious that the haircut is new, and I hate it.

—*ANONYMOUS*
COVINGTON, KENTUCKY
NUMBER OF WEDDING GUESTS: 100

WITH THIS RING, I THEE WED

The oldest historical mention of the exchange of rings during a marriage ceremony dates back nearly 5,000 years, to ancient Egypt. In those days, brides didn't sport three-karat diamonds; bands were more likely to be made of braided reeds. Wedding rings evolved over time: Romans used bands of iron, and 3,000 years after the appearance of the ring in Egypt, puzzle rings—with interlinking symbols—appeared in Asia. Poesy rings were popular during the Renaissance, while Victorians were fond of embellishing their rings with hearts and flowers, and Edwardians were partial to delicate filigree.

Wedding rings took a brief hiatus during the time of the Puritans, who felt rings were frivolous and therefore banned them. During Colonial times, it was deemed acceptable for the bride and groom to exchange wedding thimbles. Thimbles were a practical, and therefore acceptable, gift. But brides took to cutting the bottoms off those thimbles and wore them as rings. So much for practicality.

The tradition of placing the wedding band on the fourth finger of the left hand dates back to earliest recorded history. That finger was thought to contain the *venas amoris*, an artery leading directly to the heart. During medieval times, it was the custom for the groom to slide the ring halfway onto the bride's thumb, followed by her index finger, then her middle finger—signifying the Father, the Son, and the Holy Ghost—before landing on her ring finger. For Elizabethans, the thumb was the finger of choice, and in the Jewish tradition the ring is placed on the bride's index finger, because this is the finger she uses to point to the Torah.

In America, the custom of men wearing wedding bands is a fairly new one. The practice became popular during World War II, when American men started wearing rings as a reminder of the wives they left at home.

There wasn't a question about how I would do my hair: I have a shaved head.

—*JOHN MCCARTHY*
  TALLAHASSEE,
  FLORIDA
  NUMBER OF WED-
  DING GUESTS: 30

THE MODERN BRIDE doesn't have to wear white. Wear a color that makes you happy. I tried on white wedding dresses and I thought they made me look fatter. My mother was horrified that I didn't want to wear white, and my husband-to-be was upset, too. But, in the end I chose a dress with sheaths of red satin. When I walked down the aisle there was a collective gasp of surprise from our guests. I think it made a really big impression. Everyone came over to me after the ceremony and said I looked beautiful and the dress was amazing.

—*AMY*
  NEW YORK, NEW YORK

Bank On It: Money-Saving Tips

I t's a fact: *The cost of weddings is rising every year. But that does-n't mean you or your family should create a rising mountain of wedding debt to match. As we found out, there are plenty of ways to cut corners on your wedding—without cutting quality or quantity. You just have to get creative, roll up your sleeves, and do a little work yourself. Read on to discover unique ways to save money on flowers, invitations, wedding favors, food, and more.*

AS MY MOTHER ONCE SAID, "It's far better to have a small wedding followed by a big marriage, rather than the other way around."

—*RACHEL GREENE BALDINO*
SHREWSBURY, MASSACHUSETTS

DON'T GO INTO DEBT. YOUR WEDDING IS A TIME TO CELEBRATE, BUT IT'S ONLY ONE DAY.

—*BECKY HOUK*
INDIANAPOLIS, INDIANA
NUMBER OF WEDDING GUESTS: 300

FROM THE EXPERT:
PICKING UP THE CHECK

Even if the trend is to split the guest list evenly, there's no corresponding move to split the expenses. Traditionally, the bride's parents foot the bill. And frankly, even if the groom's parents offer to share the cost, the bride's parents, for the most part, graciously decline the offer. For some families the wedding is a financial stretch, in which case dividing the costs works very well and is perfectly acceptable. If this is the case, the groom's family pays half; less frequently, they'll cover music, flowers, and photography specifically. And more and more often, the bride and groom pay for their own wedding. These couples are usually older and used to doing things their own way, as well as paying for it.

SHOP WHOLESALE WHENEVER POSSIBLE. I bought all of the paper and supplies for our wedding invitations, the wedding program, place cards and menus at a paper wholesaler. I bought candles and vases for the centerpieces on clearance. The flowers were purchased through a wholesaler. One of my husband's childhood friends is a wine distributor and helped us purchase wines that were delicious and affordable.

—*MELISSA*
TACOMA, WASHINGTON
NUMBER OF WEDDING GUESTS: 110

IF YOU HAVE THE RECEPTION at a place that allows you to buy and bring your own beer and liquor, do it. I know we saved several hundred dollars by doing that.

—*JOHN KEVELTY*
WATTS FLATS, NEW YORK
NUMBER OF WEDDING GUESTS: 150

TO SAVE MONEY, my daughter held her wedding at a banquet hall the Sunday before Thanksgiving, which allowed her to negotiate for lower prices because the weekend was not as popular.

> —*SUE*
> *VERNON HILLS, ILLINOIS*
> *NUMBER OF WEDDING GUESTS: 175*

There's no reason to have napkins engraved with your name and wedding date. People are going to wipe their mouths and blow their noses in them. Just get regular, colored napkins: they will serve the purpose and cost next to nothing.

> —*MARGARET SLUSSER*
> *KENNEDY, NEW YORK*
> *NUMBER OF WEDDING GUESTS: 75*

DON'T ASSUME YOU'RE SAFE just because you hire someone you know to cater your wedding. This woman, who was great friends with my mom, ended up charging us $6,000 for food when, in actuality, the cost should have been between $2,000 and $3,000. Even worse, she took the leftovers and had a party with her friends the next day.

> —*R.W.*
> *FORT COLLINS, COLORADO*
> *NUMBER OF WEDDING GUESTS: 20*

TO SAVE MONEY ON YOUR DRESS, look for a line by a designer that has been discontinued. I saved about $600 on my dress that way.

—*KRISTINA*
SAN ANTONIO, TEXAS
NUMBER OF WEDDING GUESTS: 60

• • • • • • • •

"Want to really save money on your wedding? Don't invite anyone else! My wife and I went to Disney World—just the two of us—to get married. Then we hosted a family picnic when we got home."

—*M.R.*
HELLERTOWN, PENNSYLVANIA
NUMBER OF WEDDING GUESTS: 0

• • • • • • • •

ONE WAY TO SAVE MONEY is to trade services. One bride I know traded her services as a Web site designer for a photographer's services at her wedding. The important thing to remember is to do this only with professionals. Aunt Sally who bakes cakes for the church bake sale may not be qualified to make your 200+ person wedding cake.

—*ANN SAAVEDRA*
WALNUT CREEK, CALIFORNIA

WHO PAYS?

I'M ALL FOR THE STANDARD TRADITIONS. The groom, or his family, pays for the alcohol at the reception and everything involved with the rehearsal dinner. The bride's dad pays for everything else.

> —*C.M.*
> *PITTSBURGH, PENNSYLVANIA*
> *NUMBER OF WEDDING GUESTS: 200*

• • • • • • • • •

WE PAID FOR OUR ENTIRE WEDDING OURSELVES, and we did it without creating any additional debt. We both owned our own homes, so when I sold mine, I took a little bit of the profit to help pay for it. But mostly we saved like crazy. I quit shopping almost entirely (except for necessities) for over a year. We also didn't take any vacations that year, making the honeymoon all the sweeter. Every extra penny we saved went into a wedding account.

> —*ANONYMOUS*
> *NEW YORK, NEW YORK*
> *NUMBER OF WEDDING GUESTS: 105*

WE HAD NO PHOTOGRAPHER, no caterer, no band, and no florist, and our wedding was great. Our friends and family took pictures, we made all the food, my husband made a wedding file of music on his MP3 player, we bought some bulk roses from Costco, and my mother mixed those with wildflowers she picked and arranged them in her collection of antique pitchers.

> —*L.D.*
> *GREENVILLE, NORTH CAROLINA*
> *NUMBER OF WEDDING GUESTS: 170*

INEXPENSIVE INVITES

THE INVITATIONS WERE ONE AREA where we figured we could really save some cash. All you are really doing is trying to find out who the heck is coming so you can plan accordingly. It shouldn't cost an arm and a leg. We just bought postcards on the Internet with pictures of Aruba, our honeymoon destination, and sent them, telling people to either call or e-mail by a certain date if they could come. I'll bet we saved $400 by doing it that way.

> —*ARIC MECHLIN*
> *WATTS FLATS, NEW YORK*
> *NUMBER OF WEDDING GUESTS: 100*

MY WIFE AND I PRINTED COPIES OF OUR MOST recent studio photo together on our home printer and mailed them out as invitations with the information on the other side. It's sort of egotistical and self-promoting, but what the heck.

> —*MICHAEL JOPLING*
> *GERRY, NEW YORK*
> *NUMBER OF WEDDING GUESTS: 175*

WE DECIDED TO SAVE A BUNDLE AND send out all our invitations by e-mail. No paying for invitations, no paying for envelopes, no paying for stamps, no paying for handling. And people get them quicker and respond quicker.

> —*SEAN ABBOTT*
> *FRANKFORT, KENTUCKY*
> *NUMBER OF WEDDING GUESTS: 100*

WE HAD A VERY INFORMAL WEDDING, and I wanted my invitations to reflect that, even though all the books said that the invitations were the one place where the etiquette had to be followed to the letter. Says who? I went to the craft store and bought a couple of packages of homemade paper and a couple of rolls of very thin ribbon. Then I printed the invitations six to a page on some of the paper and cut the rest into four squares a page. Then I cut the invitations and tied the printed part to the larger squares I had cut with the ribbon I had bought. They were all different, and so pretty. The best part was that the whole thing cost me about $22. And guess what? The sky didn't fall!

—B.R.
CHAPEL HILL, NORTH CAROLINA
NUMBER OF WEDDING GUESTS: 70

WHO PAYS?

When it comes to weddings, tradition has it that the bride's family picks up the tab for the event. There are, however, certain financial responsibilities that fall to all members of the wedding party. Below is a quick guide.

What the bride pays for:
- Groom's wedding ring and gift
- Gifts for the maid of honor and bridesmaids
- Wedding dress (and accessories)
- Wedding consultant

What the groom pays for:
- Bride's engagement and wedding rings, and gift
- Gifts for the best man and ushers
- Marriage license
- Officiant's fee
- Tuxedo
- Boutonnieres
- The honeymoon

What the bride's family pays for:
- Invitations and announcements
- Transportation for the bridal party
- The reception
- Flowers for the wedding, including bouquets for the bride and her attendants
- Photographer and/or videography
- DJ or band

What the groom's family pays for:
- Rehearsal dinner
- Flowers to be worn by immediate family members

What the attendants pay for:
- Cost of dress or tuxedo
- Travel expenses if the wedding is out of town
- Gift for the bride and groom
- Bride's attendants pay for the bridal shower and bachelorette party
- Groom's attendants pay for the bachelor party

FROM THE EXPERT:
MORE FUN, LESS EXPENSIVE

My favorite strategy for couples on a limited budget is this: Have a cocktail reception instead of a sit-down dinner.

- Find a date for a Thursday or Friday evening, or a Sunday at 4 o'clock in the afternoon: Saturday-night space rentals often come with a premium price tag.
- Make sure your invitation reads, "Please join us for our wedding at 5:00 p.m.; cocktail reception to follow until 9:00 p.m." Give a start and an end time.
- Set up cocktail tables, or even some 42˝ tables, which are slightly larger, to handle about half the crowd; not everyone can sit down at the same time, but the tables are constantly cleared as people get up.
- You have music and dancing from the very beginning, right after the ceremony.
- Servers pass an abundance of hors d'oeuvres, and fork-and-finger-food buffets are set up around the room.
- Then you do the cake cutting ceremony and pass pieces of cake, offer demitasse coffee, petits fours, and long-stemmed, chocolate-covered strawberries—what more could you ask for?

The phrase "cocktail reception" lets guests know they can go out to dinner afterward. But in reality you give them so much food that nobody is going to go out to dinner, much less go home hungry.

You save expense and time by eliminating all those big tables, settings, centerpieces, place cards, and long tablecloths. The champagne's flowing, there's dancing and fun. It really works! That's absolutely my favorite kind of wedding.

HEADLINES
Best Advice and Top Tips

- Don't let other people tell you what kind of wedding to have.

- Delegate responsibility; ask others to take care of tasks that are less important to you.

- Remember to take time to relax and *stop* thinking about your wedding.

- Try to tackle one project at a time so that you don't get over-whelmed.

- Set aside at least one night every week for you and your fiancé or fiancée to spend some quality time together.

WHEN DEALING WITH MY IN-LAWS during wedding planning, I spoke through my husband. When you disagree with your own parent over details, it's OK, but it's not comfortable to do with somebody else's parent. The decision to deal with our own parents was smart—it helped keep the peace!

—CARA M. RAICH
NEW YORK, NEW YORK
NUMBER OF WEDDING GUESTS: 200

• • • • • • • •

PLAN YOUR OWN WEDDING; don't rely on your parents to do it for you. I was in college at the time, so my mom did most of the work. I wish I could replan everything. It was your typical church wedding—way too traditional. This was OK, but there was really nothing in the ceremony or reception that made it our own.

—ELIZABETH
FORT WAYNE, INDIANA
NUMBER OF WEDDING GUESTS: 200

WE SPENT MORE NIGHTS at the local comedy club while we were planning the wedding than you would believe. Laughing always makes you feel better and less stressed. It got to the point where most of the staff in the club knew us by first name. Anytime we started getting short with each other, one of us would say, "let's go," and that night we'd hit the club.

> —*ANONYMOUS*
> *GERRY, NEW YORK*
> *NUMBER OF WEDDING GUESTS: 100*

. . . .

IF I COULD DO IT ALL OVER, I would not allow others to manipulate the plans so much. I felt immense pressure from our families (his and mine) to have this big bash and allow them to invite whomever they wanted. If we had done things my way, it would have been a much smaller affair, and we could have afforded a nice sit-down dinner and live music.

> —*KATIE*
> *DALLAS, TEXAS*
> *NUMBER OF WEDDING GUESTS: 400*

. . . .

MY HUSBAND AND I WERE HAPPY to have our parents help out as much as possible. It really helped us deal with the stress and the fact that we live very far from our wedding venue. My fiancé's father knew we loved jazz and wanted a jazz band to play at the wedding. He found a local, Pittsburgh-based band that played at events and met with them, saw them perform at a local venue, and hired them. He sent us a CD prior to signing the contract, which we listened to and enjoyed very much, and we gave our approval.

> —*JENNIFER AGNEW*
> *LOS ANGELES, CALIFORNIA*
> *NUMBER OF WEDDING GUESTS: 98*

Your ability to laugh will do more good for you than a hot stone massage.

—*REBEKAH MITCHELL*
FORT WORTH,
TEXAS
NUMBER OF WED-
DING GUESTS: 300

OUR WEDDING WAS CERTAINLY the wedding my parents never got to have, and they took over as much as we'd allow. Our attitude: at least we're not paying. We tried to be relaxed about the details and just picked a few things we cared about: clothes, cakes and the band. The dinner was something we would never have chosen, for example, but we just let it slide!

—*JULIE*
AUSTIN, TEXAS
NUMBER OF WEDDING GUESTS: 315

• • • • • • • •

TO MAKE THE TASK EASIER, I would concentrate on one thing per week, because you can't do everything all at once. One week I would call the florists and make appointments to see them. The next week I might go on those appointments and start looking at bakeries for the cake. I had a year, so I spaced it out and organized it. This way, I never got too stressed out, and I got to relax in the last month knowing that everything was taken care of.

—*WENDY*
ALLENTOWN, PENNSYLVANIA
NUMBER OF WEDDING GUESTS: 140

• • • • • • • •

DURING MY WEDDING PLANNING I decreased stress by letting others take care of the things that did not really matter to me. My mom kept asking, "What about this? What about that?" I would reply to her, "If you want me to have a cake, then you can order one and bring it. If you want me to have engraved napkins, then you can buy some and bring them." I really did not care about these details so I just let others handle it.

—*TIFFANY*
OKLAHOMA CITY, OKLAHOMA
NUMBER OF WEDDING GUESTS: 40-50

FIND SOMETHING YOU CAN DO with your fiancé during the planning process that gives you dedicated time together. We signed up for ballroom dancing lessons: In addition to having a whole dance made up for us, we had 10 guaranteed dates during a very stressful, busy time of wedding planning. It was a lot of fun for both of us.

—*MARCELLE HENDRICKS*
WESTMINSTER, COLORADO
NUMBER OF WEDDING GUESTS: 200

"Find time to *stop* thinking about your wedding. There are so many details, your head will spin. I'd go out and exercise. Ironically, that's when I thought of the best ideas for my wedding. "

—*AMY JEFFERY*
BRIDGTON, MAINE
NUMBER OF WEDDING GUESTS: 100

I REMEMBER PUTTING MY REALLY SMALL budget into this Web site that was supposed to help with this stuff, and it came back saying I should spend $300 on flowers and $27 on the groom's suit. We can get married without flowers, but a naked groom would be a little embarrassing!

—*S.G.*
SEATTLE, WASHINGTON
NUMBER OF WEDDING GUESTS: 35

GET ORGANIZED!

KEEP A SMALL NOTEBOOK AT YOUR SIDE every moment for recording that great idea that may pop up. Get an accordion folder for every photo, article, or subject that may inspire you. Keep budget, vendor contracts, and price list comparisons filed here as well.

> —*ANONYMOUS*
> *LONG VALLEY, NEW JERSEY*

MY FIANCÉ AND I CHOSE ONE NIGHT out of the week to discuss what we both wanted in our wedding. This way, you both are not burned out on wedding planning, you both have a better idea of what you want in the wedding, and you both are less overwhelmed by the whole process. And you both learn how to communicate, which will help you out later in your marriage.

> —*STEPHANIE TORTORICI*
> *BIRMINGHAM, ALABAMA*
> *NUMBER OF WEDDING GUESTS: 300*

STAY AS ORGANIZED AS POSSIBLE. I would try so hard not to pile up hundreds of bridal magazines, so I tore out anything that would catch my eye. Then I threw out the magazine. I created my own wedding planner with a binder and labeled divider tabs. It was so organized; I knew exactly what I was looking for.

> —*JESSICA CARLIN*
> *NEW YORK, NEW YORK*
> *NUMBER OF WEDDING GUESTS: 150*

BRIDES AND THEIR MOTHERS RUN the show completely when it comes to weddings. It is the girl's big day. But my mother had been on the other side before—my brother had gotten married two years before I did—and she didn't want to treat my husband's mother the way she felt she was treated in that wedding. So we went out of our way to include my mother-in-law in practically all the planning. Just remember, you might be on the other side one day. So treat your mother-in-law the way you would hope your own son's wife and mother-in-law would treat you. It's the golden rule.

> —LORNA MERKEIL
> ELLSWORTH, OHIO
> NUMBER OF WEDDING GUESTS: 150

Don't sweat the small (or even big) stuff!

> —TRACY BROWN WRIGHT
> GAINESVILLE, FLORIDA
> NUMBER OF WEDDING GUESTS: 100

• • • • • • • •

ALLOW FOR EMERGENCIES. Your invitations may come in late, the calligrapher's dog may get sick, your dyed-to-match shoes may shrink during the process, and the adorable party favors you ordered may be delivered in the wrong color. Give yourself extra time so that minor set-backs do not cause hysteria.

> —CHERYL K.
> BROOKLYN, NEW YORK

• • • • • • • •

FOLLOW YOUR INSTINCTS when planning your wedding. Instead of doing what they want, most women do what their parents, and their fiancé's parents, want. My fiancé and I were careful to come to our own decisions about things first, then take those choices to our families, saying, "Here's what we decided. Would you like to help?"

> —PAULA
> WESTPORT, CONNECTICUT
> NUMBER OF WEDDING GUESTS: 11

YOU SHOULD TREAT PLANNING the wedding like running a business. My fiancé used to send me Web links on e-mail and they'd get lost. For this reason, we set up a system of communication and worked out what's high priority and how long things should take to review, etc. This helps alleviate some of the stress of planning.

—*ARI*
NEW YORK, NEW YORK

. . . .

"Don't forget to go out to dinner occasionally and talk about things other than the wedding. Quality time with your fiancé away from the "roses versus lilies" debate is time well spent."

—*BETH H.*
NEW YORK, NEW YORK

. . . .

TO REDUCE PRE-WEDDING STRESS, give each other massages. My husband and I started giving each other nightly massages before our wedding to calm down and reconnect each day.

—*TARA GREEN*
ATLANTA, GEORGIA
NUMBER OF WEDDING GUESTS: 120

GOOD GROOM ADVICE

WHATEVER YOUR BRIDE-TO-BE ASKS YOU ABOUT, no matter how insignificant, and no matter how little you actually care about it, think for a second and try to have an opinion.

> —*JOHN*
> *ATHENS, GEORGIA*
> *NUMBER OF WEDDING GUESTS: 200*

LET YOUR WIFE DO EVERYTHING. It's a lot of work, but it's the woman's dream day and it won't work if she doesn't like it. My role was to be supportive for whatever my wife needed.

> —*BRAENDON LINDBERG*
> *SAN ANTONIO, TEXAS*
> *NUMBER OF WEDDING GUESTS: 60*

WHEN I HAD ABOUT FIVE WEEKS until the wedding, I became a bundle of nerves. I found myself taking on the attributes of the dreaded "bridezilla"! The worst part was that I was taking out all the pressure I was feeling on the people I love most. Thankfully, my fiancé had a sense of humor about it. Still, I did not want to be so stressed out. I utilized the cycle of the year to set things right. As we approached Rosh Hashanah (the Jewish New Year) I made a conscious intention to let go of all the stress. On the holiday, I reviewed my year, looking at the events and feelings that led me to this moment, and I released all the feelings that no longer served me. This new year symbolizes new beginnings for me in many ways.

> —*JESSICA FIALKOFF*
> *MARBLETOWN, NEW YORK*
> *NUMBER OF WEDDING GUESTS: 118*

TIPS FROM THE BIG FAT GREEK WEDDING

I lived through the big fat Greek wedding! My husband is non-Greek, so we had a lot of clashing opinions, rituals, and traditions:

1. If you are the man, stay out of the planning. It's your wife's day to celebrate; you're just the icing on the cake. She's the whole cake, and then some.

2. If you're the bride, choose your battles with your mother and other family matters carefully. It's your mother's day, anyway. She's living out the wedding she never had, showing off (proudly, of course) to friends and family, and going through an emotional time of letting her little girl go. Choose something you feel strongly about—for example, the flowers—and be in charge of that. Other than that, let your mom be in charge. She'll love it.

3. Don't let people's requests and idiosyncracies get you annoyed: for example, bringing two newborns to your wedding, or bringing *their* out-of-town guests to your reception; or relatives getting bent out of shape because of your wedding date or color choice. Let it be. In the long run, it doesn't matter.

4. Enjoy your day. You'll only have one, hopefully. Put someone else in charge of the details. Make sure it's a decisive, organized, responsible person you can trust. Make a list for them, and make them take care of the details and not consult with you or your family for any questions. Then enjoy your day, and forget all the rest!

—SOPHIA MARX
SANTA CLARA, CALIFORNIA

WE CREATED A BUDGET and set up a new bank account just for wedding money. We are contributing the lion's share of the funds—we each put in a set amount each month—but our parents have all wanted to help out in some way, so when we receive support from them it goes directly into that account. This has also allowed us to avoid any one parent having decision-making power.

—KRISTIN JACOBSEN
SEATTLE, WASHINGTON

" Don't be selfish. Let your future mother-in-law do some of the work. I let mine do the cake. She's putting a fountain on it with dark red water and rose petals. It's very tacky, but I don't care. "

—KRISTINA
SAN ANTONIO, TEXAS
NUMBER OF WEDDING GUESTS: 60

LET THE PARENTS FEEL THEY'RE a big part of your wedding. Otherwise, you can create a lifetime of animosity. We invited entire families to our wedding (we had tons of kids there) and it was a massive group of disorganization. But it made our family happy and that was important to us.

—CATHERINE BROWN
LYNBROOK, NEW YORK
NUMBER OF WEDDING GUESTS: 300

WEDDING DON'TS

THE WORST THING YOU CAN DO is misspell something important on the invitations. We found that out the hard way. For us it was the name of the church. We proofread that thing over and over before it went to print, but we all missed it. Many of our guests mentioned the gaffe to us at the reception. They would all say something like, "It's no big deal, but do you realize you misspelled the name?" Well, obviously it was a big deal because they all saw it and all felt the need to tell us!

—*KIM SWIATEK*
WATTS FLATS, NEW YORK
NUMBER OF WEDDING GUESTS: 200

DON'T GET A KITTEN TWO WEEKS before your wedding: My fiancée pulled that one. We already had a dog, and then she came home with this kitten. So for several nights leading up to the wedding we got approximately two hours of sleep while the dog chased the kitten, or the kitten attacked our feet. We had the kitten on a trial run, thankfully, so we gave it back and it found a home with people who didn't need as much sleep as we did and weren't planning the biggest day of their lives.

—*J.A.*
ATLANTA, GEORGIA
NUMBER OF WEDDING GUESTS: 200

DON'T NEGLECT YOUR SPOUSE-TO-BE. Make sure you remember that the two of you are still in a relationship. Make those special dinners, clean the house, buy her flowers—treat her as if you just started dating. Doing so will relax her and get you to your wedding.

—*AARON BLANK*
SEATTLE, WASHINGTON
NUMBER OF WEDDING GUESTS: 125

FROM THE EXPERT: KEY TO SUCCESS #4 —TIMELINESS

Another behind-the-scenes tip: You want everything to happen on time. Wedding planners know how important this is. When the party doesn't keep to its schedule, you and your guests will certainly notice; when everything runs on time, you won't.

We create a timeline for all of our weddings. It gives the order of events of the wedding day, and can be very intricate, including all of the wedding details. This document is meant less as a minute-by-minute schedule than as a chronology for the day.

IF YOU ARE A CONTROL FREAK LIKE ME, you are probably going to have a nervous breakdown at some point leading up to your wedding. You are going to have no control over the interpersonal interactions that will happen at your wedding; make a conscious decision to let go. The day before my wedding, I lost it. It was mainly because my mother-in-law said something about how my mother should have done something, and I understood that I would not be able to be the social buffer that I usually am at family gatherings. All these people would be in one place, and I would have no control over what happened. My mother had to sit me down and tell me very firmly that people would look after themselves, and I had to let go or I would have a horrible time.

—*SUMMER DANIELS*
SAN FRANCISCO, CALIFORNIA
NUMBER OF WEDDING GUESTS: 95

. . . .

"Don't focus on what the wedding should be like; focus on what the marriage should be like. Wedding logistics take a lot of time, but talking about your future is so much more essential."

—*KATHLEEN PEARCE*
PORTSMOUTH, NEW HAMPSHIRE

FROM THE EXPERT: SHARING THE BURDEN

A bride can't really be her own wedding manager. Even a mother of the bride cannot do it. They have far more important functions at the wedding, and worrying about the hors d'oeuvres shouldn't be their burden.

A woman once hired me to plan her daughter's wedding. She said she'd done her own planning of an earlier event, but on the day of that party she was tearing her hair out because she had to make sure everything went just so. At her daughter's wedding she was able to have a good time and not worry. She completely enjoyed it because she let me fulfill her daughter's dreams and her own expectations for this special day.

Banquet managers can't really manage the whole wedding day. They don't know their clients well enough and they have other things on their minds, namely the interests of the venue. A wedding planner has an eye on every detail and knows very well what the bride and groom envision for their special day. Every vendor represents something; the food, the music, or something else. A wedding planner only represents the bride and groom and their interests.

Although not everyone can afford a wedding planner for the entire process, here's a tip: Hire a planner for the last four weeks. You set everything up with your vendors and then hire the wedding planner to review all of your vendor paperwork and execute every detail on the wedding day. Save yourself for your most important role— being the bride.

CONSIDER TREATING YOURSELF to a new computer in place of a personal wedding coordinator! I can't imagine planning a wedding without one.

—*ANONYMOUS*
LONG VALLEY, NEW JERSEY

• • • • • • • •

TREASURE THE TIME YOU SPEND with your mom. When will you be able to go shopping all day for the perfect dress with matching jewelry and shoes?

—*REBEKAH MITCHELL*
FORT WORTH, TEXAS
NUMBER OF WEDDING GUESTS: 300

Bring It On: Registering for Gifts

Wedding showers fall under the category of "party with a purpose." And the purpose is to help you and your spouse start off your lives in a home stocked with all the right goods. But there are some challenges: Unless you want to receive a dozen toasters, you should probably spend a few hours registering at a respectable store for everything you really want and need. You should also drop the guilt: Don't feel bad about asking for presents. Read on for more stories and tips.

AT FIRST WE THOUGHT it was tacky to ask for things, but then we realized people were grateful to be able to give us something we actually needed instead of another toaster.
—*K.B.*
SAN FRANCISCO, CALIFORNIA

REGISTER FOR *TONS*. DON'T BE SHY.
—*SUSAN*
CHICAGO, ILLINOIS

FROM THE EXPERT: SHOWERS

Showers have traditionally been planned as a luncheon party, but one trend in the past few years has been to make it a tea, at 3 o'clock in the afternoon, on a Saturday or a Sunday. Most showers are general, but some have themes. For example, guests are given a time of day; cocktails or breakfast is popular. Gifts are chosen with that in mind. And naturally, if you go to a wedding shower and bring a shower gift, you are still expected to send a wedding gift for the wedding. It can become an expensive proposition.

I TOLD THE PLANNERS OF MY WEDDING SHOWER to tell me when the shower was, but not to tell me the details. That was a good decision: I showed up and was very excited to see everyone and celebrate with them at a restaurant near my mother's home. I think you should trust the people who are hosting it for you. If you know too much, you'll have opinions and start changing the plans. Your shower is supposed to be a gift; you don't need to organize it.

—DORI
NEW YORK, NEW YORK
NUMBER OF WEDDING GUESTS: 250

• • • • • • • • •

MAKE SURE YOU REGISTER AT ONE PLACE that has a brick-and-mortar store near at least some of the guests. Some people like to go in and see what they're getting you, wrap it themselves, bring it with them to the wedding, and/or save on the shipping fees. Also, make sure you register at one online place, because a lot of other people will just want to have it done quickly and painlessly.

—ANNE B.
SAN FRANCISCO, CALIFORNIA

THINGS TO DO

4 WEEKS BEFORE YOUR WEDDING

_____Apply for your marriage license.

_____Have your final gown fitting. Have your maid of honor come with you to learn how to bustle your train and fasten any tricky buttons.

_____Confirm that your bridesmaids and groomsmen have their attire, and confirm their arrival times on the big day.

_____Confirm arrival times with all your vendors.

_____Print your wedding program.

_____If you'll be changing your name and/or address after the wedding, notify the post office, Social Security Administration, banks, etc.

_____If you've received gifts from those unable to attend the wedding, send your thank-you notes.

_____Have your mother or maid of honor get in touch with any guests who have not sent an RSVP.

1 TO 2 WEEKS BEFORE YOUR WEDDING

_____Make your seating plan and write out place cards.

_____Give a final head count to your caterer.

_____Write toasts for the rehearsal dinner and reception.

_____Break in your wedding shoes by wearing them on carpeted surfaces around the house.

_____Make arrangements for someone to water your plants, pick up your mail and/or care for your pet while you are on your honeymoon.

_____Pick up your wedding dress.

_____Give a family member a copy of your honeymoon itinerary in case of emergency.

THE DAY BEFORE YOUR WEDDING

_____Give each member of your wedding party a specific responsibility: handing out corsages and boutonnieres, greeting and seating guests, accepting gifts, checking on vendors, etc.

_____Confirm your transportation.

_____Give your wedding party their gifts.

_____Have a manicure, pedicure, or a massage, and relax!

GROOMS & SHOWERS

ACT LIKE YOU CARE ABOUT THINGS that are important to her: She won't care if you're pretending and will actually appreciate your effort. It is called caring.

> —*TED RINEY*
> *DALLAS, TEXAS*
> *NUMBER OF WEDDING GUESTS: 300*

• • • • • • • • •

GET YOUR HUSBAND-TO-BE TO REGISTER WITH YOU—he has to live with the stuff, too, so he might as well like it. And register at places that have things he wants, too. My fiancé picked out a cordless drill, a stepladder and luggage, and was very excited to receive them as gifts.

> —*MARCELLE HENDRICKS*
> *WESTMINSTER, COLORADO*
> *NUMBER OF WEDDING GUESTS: 200*

• • • • • • • • •

WHEN YOUR BRIDE HAS HER FIRST SHOWER, order a dozen red roses and have them hand-delivered to the shower. Also, get six roses, pink preferred, and have them delivered to the mother of the bride and, of course, to your mom. What better way to get on the good side of your bride, your moms, and all the females in attendance? Then show up at the end of the shower and make sure you help carry all those presents to the car. Your wife will always remember that.

> —*AARON BLANK*
> *SEATTLE, WASHINGTON*

Last Moments of Freedom: Bachelor & Bachelorette Parties

*P*arties that celebrate the waning days of singledom for both the bride and groom can run the gamut of events—from the traditional (including visitations with paid members of the opposite sex) to the adventurous (fishing and hiking, anyone?) to the calming (i.e., alone time). What kind of party you choose largely depends on the reaction of your future spouse when you announce your plans—at least, that's what we advise. Read on for stories about how others enjoyed their final single days.

SET TWO WEEKENDS ASIDE before your wedding. Spend the first with just your friends, saying goodbye to the days when you guys would hang out together without her. Spend the second completely alone contemplating the step you're about to take. Your mind clears up real fast this way.

—ANTHONY MANUEL
KINDER, LOUISIANA
NUMBER OF WEDDING GUESTS: 20

WE HAD ONE RULE ABOUT THE BACHE-LOR PARTY: No NAKED WOMEN.

—M.W.
KIRKLAND, WASHINGTON

HEAD LINES
Best Advice and Top Tips

- Don't have your bachelor or bachelorette party the night before the wedding. You'll both be in better shape to handle the ceremony the next day.

- Make sure you clear any plans for strippers with your future spouse so as not to start your new life together on the wrong foot.

- Think of alternatives to the traditional bachelor and bachelorette parties: go on a shopping spree, plan a fishing trip, or visit a spa with your close friends.

- Cherish your last celebration with your friends before you embark on your new life.

- If you're planning a wild party, consider holding it out of town, so you don't run into any of your future spouse's friends.

IF YOU'RE GOING TO HAVE A BACHELORETTE (or bachelor) party, make sure you know how your soon-to-be-spouse feels about strippers and flirting. My friend's husband told me that he would not go through with his wedding if there were male strippers at her party. So I got a friend of mine to *pretend* to be a stripper; he came in dancing with some sexy music on, but it was quickly apparent he wasn't a real stripper. And then he spent the entire song just trying to get his cowboy boots off. It cracked us all up.

—*JEAN*
MINNEAPOLIS, MINNESOTA

I THINK THAT IF YOU'RE REALLY READY to settle down, and you truly love your woman, you won't feel the urge to have a "traditional" bachelor party with massive amounts of alcohol and strippers. My friends and I simply got together for a casual round of drinks—I barely even remember it. Much more important was showing respect for my future wife.

—*ROBERT SALTER*
MÖNCHENGLADBACH, GERMANY
NUMBER OF WEDDING GUESTS: 100

"Make sure you stay up talking all through the night, in your pajamas, drinking a bottle of wine with your best friends and roommates. You'll be amazed at how much fun that sounds in later years."

—*K.C.*
SAN FRANCISCO, CALIFORNIA

GO TO VEGAS. MY BEST MAN and two cars full of friends drove me to Vegas for our bachelor weekend. Great place to have a bachelor party; the town was meant for it. Everything you want all in one spot: nightclubs, gambling, drinking, strippers, great food, and cheap hotels!

—*J.K.*
LOS ANGELES, CALIFORNIA
NUMBER OF WEDDING GUESTS: 240

LEG IS BROKEN, HEART IS NOT

I chose what I thought would be a nice, wholesome bachelor party: a day of canoeing and fishing (and bourbon) on my favorite river. My dad was best man, a sober designated driver, a burger chef, and in charge of the boats, and that left me free to fish and drink whiskey with eight to 10 good buddies.

The day went great. We all got drunk and sunburned and caught as many fish as we could. We stopped at a nice floodplain field to eat and play football. On the field, I was faster than I'd ever been; I was outrunning a friend who had won a track scholarship. Then, I lined up on defense, ran the pattern backwards, stepped in a hole, and, due to blazing speed and drunkenness, completely shattered the tip of my fibula. It was loud and hurt like hell.

It was hard to admit that I wasn't going to walk this one off, but I just decided to lie on the picnic table and wait for the boys to finish the game, eat, sober up, and then I'd catch a ride into the emergency room. But I knew I'd have to call my bride-to-be and tell her the news. I was very scared, but it went better than expected; she was more concerned *about* me than upset *at* me.

A friend gave me this advice: No matter how stressful things could get during the actual day, we had already put enough effort and energy into it that things will happen. His examples of things that will happen were more along the lines of not moving the flowers from the church to the reception, or making sure Aunt Betty's dishes don't get mixed up with the caterer's. But the same can be said of a broken leg. I had a lot of duties, and they all involved driving, but all of a sudden I couldn't drive. But people helped, and it was really fun.

—JOHN
ATHENS, GEORGIA
NUMBER OF WEDDING GUESTS: 200

OUR BACHELOR AND BACHELORETTE PARTIES were the weekend of the wedding. I was a tad scared about my husband's bachelor party, in case there were any "accidents"—chipped teeth, cuts, etc. He made it through OK, but you never know. If you have a wild party, make sure there's enough time to fix anything that might happen.

> —ADRIANE
> DAVIE, FLORIDA

· · · · · · · ·

MY BACHELORETTE PARTY was actually a weekend at a spa: classy dinners, massages, and a little harmless drinking and flirting at the bar at night. It was an expensive way to go, but it meant there were only a few of my closest friends and cousins with me. It was great.

> —A.B.
> SAN FRANCISCO, CALIFORNIA

· · · · · · · ·

I DIDN'T WANT THE KIND OF bachelorette party you see in the movies. I didn't need to get drunk. I just wanted something to help me celebrate my last days as a single person and transition to a new phase in life. So I went on a retreat with several of my closest friends, where we did yoga, had some quiet time to think, ate well, had long conversations, and took some beautiful walks in the woods. It was lovely and peaceful.

> —E.C.
> SAN FRANCISCO, CALIFORNIA
> NUMBER OF WEDDING GUESTS: 80

Bachelor party on a boat: Good idea for fishing and fun, bad idea if you're going to get rip-roaring drunk and have a tendency to get seasick!

—SAM
SANTA MONICA, CALIFORNIA

HEADLINES
Best Advice and Top Tips

- Include in your rehearsal friends and relatives who weren't asked to be in your wedding party. It's a way to make them feel special.

- Even if you keep the rehearsal dinner small, invite everyone attending the wedding to join you for coffee and dessert afterward.

- You may enjoy the rehearsal more than the actual wedding because you're likely to be more relaxed.

- Be prepared to hear a lot of speeches at your rehearsal dinner—some of which may embarrass you!

- Consider having the rehearsal dinner a few nights before the wedding, rather than the night before—it will give you more time to relax and take care of any last-minute tasks before the big day.

PREPARE TO BE EMBARRASSED at your rehearsal dinner. I'm fortunate that my friends are generous-hearted and smart guys. There was one moment, however, when I would have paid someone to put a bullet in my head. My mom had some old dude in Nashville write a song about me and my wife that incorporated biographical information about us. Apparently, this is the guy's craft. There was nothing about the song's content that was humiliating—it was just the scene of us sitting there in the dining room in awkward silence listening to this creepy jingle about us play over the PA system: I shudder even now.

—*ANONYMOUS*
BLUEFIELD, WEST VIRGINIA
NUMBER OF WEDDING GUESTS: 175

IT'S TRADITIONAL TO DO THE REHEARSAL the night before the wedding, but we decided to do it a couple of nights before. For one thing, I wanted to have the day and night before the wedding to myself in case there were last-minute things that needed taking care of. Also, I didn't want people to be drinking at the rehearsal and then be hungover for the wedding. This way, people could have a good time without worrying that the wedding was the next day.

—*RACHAEL JACKSON*
DRY RIDGE, KENTUCKY
NUMBER OF WEDDING GUESTS: 160

• • • • • • • •

DON'T CONFUSE THE REHEARSAL DINNER with a family dinner. The rehearsal is intended just for the wedding party, the minister, and your parents. You are not expected to pay for a dinner for all your friends and family. You'll be doing that the next night. One of my brothers-in-law complained that he wasn't invited to the rehearsal and I told him he could eat twice as much at the wedding if it made him feel better.

—*LEAH GERSON*
ZIRKLE, VIRGINIA

• • • • • • • •

MAKE BETS WITH YOUR PROSPECTIVE SPOUSE about certain people: which relative will have the gall to wear white to the wedding and which to wear red; who will be the first person to spill red wine down the front of their clothes; the first to get drunk; the first to do the worm on the dance floor; the first to fall down. It helps take the pressure off.

—*SUE GRANT*
GREENFORD, OHIO
NUMBER OF WEDDING GUESTS: 200

IN CASE WORDS FAIL YOU

Looking for just the right words? Poemsforfree .com offers 1,500 poems, all written by the same person and each dealing with special occasions.

FROM THE EXPERT: THE REHEARSAL—DO IT TWICE

You do the ceremony rehearsal so that the members of the wedding party don't feel like morons and don't look like morons during your actual wedding ceremony. Sometimes brides would like to dispense with a rehearsal but you *must* have the rehearsal, and that's that. We go through everything once, we show everyone what to do, and then we do it again, so that they know exactly what they're doing and when, and so that they're comfortable with what they're doing.

It often happens that this is the first event for friends and relatives who haven't seen each other for quite a while. I always fudge the call time for a rehearsal. For example, if the rehearsal is scheduled at 5:00 p.m. with the venue, I have the bride tell her entire wedding party that the rehearsal is scheduled at 4:30. This way, between late arrivals and chatty people, the rehearsal itself is bound to begin on time.

WE HAD TOO MANY GOOD FRIENDS and relatives to include all of them in our wedding party or ceremony. So we used the rehearsal dinner to let some older relatives and friends feel like they were an important part of the weekend. We asked them to do specific things, such as give a speech, make a toast, sing a song, or help us greet people.

—*Luz*
San Diego, California
Number of wedding guests: 220

EVEN THOUGH YOU'LL BE BURNED OUT from planning the actual wedding, make sure you plan the rehearsal dinner, too. We just couldn't muster the energy to make yet another seating plan for the rehearsal dinner, and it ended up being a mess. For example, one of my young friends got isolated in the midst of my wife's older relatives with hearing problems!

—*FRANK*
RENO, NEVADA
NUMBER OF WEDDING GUESTS: 90

. . . .

"Our rehearsal dinner was more fun than the wedding. For one thing, we were more relaxed."

—*MARIA*
BROOKLYN, NEW YORK
NUMBER OF WEDDING GUESTS: 100

. . . .

AT OUR REHEARSAL DINNER, one of my husband's friends got up and spontaneously delivered the most inappropriate speech ever—about my husband's past girlfriends! I don't know how you could prevent this sort of thing, but maybe you should have somebody on alert to help out in such "emergencies." I wish somebody had just sat him down and made some joke to ease the tension.

—*K.C.*
SAN FRANCISCO, CALIFORNIA

DINNER DIPLOMACY

My husband's mother and stepfather offered to host the rehearsal dinner. But they had a different idea of what type of event it should be and how many people should be invited. Based on etiquette books and a general desire to be inclusive, my mom and I were very insistent that the party include all family as well as all out-of-town guests. The hitch was that I had a lot more family and a lot more out-of-town guests there. We talked them into having a more informal meal at the small hotel we had taken over for our out-of-towners. But the real stumbling block was my husband's father. My husband's mother did *not* want to invite him to the party (they are divorced). She

figured she was hosting so she could decide whom to invite and not invite. They can barely stand to be in the same room together. I thought my mother handled this brilliantly. She basically took the tack of attributing only good motives to her. It went something along the lines of, "I *know* that you feel—as I do—that the kids' fathers are important to them and need to be included regardless of our feelings about them. I mean, it's only one day, and I know what a generous person you are . . . I know you will invite your ex-husband, even though he doesn't deserve it, etc." It worked: She said, "Yes, of course." And that was that.

—ANONYMOUS
WASHINGTON, D.C.
NUMBER OF WEDDDING GUESTS: 150

FROM THE EXPERT: WATCH THE DRINKING

Be very cautious about drinking at the rehearsal dinner and on the wedding day. That caution goes double for the bride and groom. At your rehearsal dinner, keep in mind that a hangover is no way to start your wedding day.

I always urge the best man not to drink at the wedding. If he drinks too much he's going to say things he shouldn't say. He's going to embarrass the groom, he'll embarrass himself—it happens! I've seen it too often. People make fools of themselves all the time.

WE HAD A LOT OF FILIPINO RELATIVES in the wedding who didn't speak English too well, if at all, so we did a very careful, bilingual run-through and enlisted some of the younger, more bilingual folks to help the older people. If you don't have enough bilingual people to make it all run smoothly, I think it would be worth it to hire a few.

—*JULIE*
SAN FRANCISCO, CALIFORNIA

* * * * * * * *

AFTER THE REHEARSAL AND DINNER ARE OVER, open up your rehearsal dinner to everybody. About 30 extra people came for dessert and coffee. It wasn't too expensive for my parents, and it was so nice to be able to visit with those people. Lord knows we didn't get to do much actual visiting on the day of the wedding!

—*SHANNON*
SAN RAFAEL, CALIFORNIA

I was worried about the veil and not being able to pull it up during the wedding. So my fiancée and I used the veil during the rehearsal so that I'd have a chance to deal with it.

—*NORT ADAMEK*
FRANKFORT, KENTUCKY
NUMBER OF WEDDING GUESTS: 50

FROM THE EXPERT: REHEARSAL DINNER—TIME FOR SPEECHES

The only speeches that should be given on the wedding day are the welcome given by the parents, and from the best man and maid or matron of honor. All other speeches should be given at the rehearsal dinner. Sometimes these speeches go on too long. Tell everyone to speak for two minutes, expecting that they'll speak for five. Most people respect that. At one wedding, a best man rambled on for what felt like hours. I kept saying to myself, "Oh, my God, get the hook!" It got to the point that I had to ask the groom to put an end to the guests' misery!

Plan something that doesn't end up in a bar if you want yourself, your guests, and your future husband to be feeling their best on the big day.

—D.M.
CORTE MADERA, CALIFORNIA
NUMBER OF WEDDING GUESTS: 190

OUR REHEARSAL DINNER was filled with awkward speeches as well as nice speeches. But the fun part began afterward—when we all wandered over to the hotel bar. That's when everyone loosened up and my friends hung out with my bride's friends and really got to know each other. I remember at one point playing a game called Suck & Blow, where you take a driver's license, suck it onto your lips, and then pass it to the next person at the table, blowing it onto their lips as they suck. Talk about something that really brings people close together! There's always the groomsman who "accidentally" drops the driver's license just before he passes it to the pretty bridesmaid, so that their lips "accidentally" come together. Once the wedding day came around, all our friends were acting like old friends.

—J.A.
ATLANTA, GEORGIA
NUMBER OF WEDDING GUESTS: 200

The Biggest Day of Your Life: How to Prepare

Tequila. Cartoons. A nap. Xanax. A checklist. Pick your poison, you'll probably use one to calm your nerves and help you get ready on your wedding day. After all, you're facing one of the most stressful times of your life: You, giving your life away to another, in front of a crowd of people. And to top it off, tradition says you're not even allowed to see the one person who can calm you down: your future spouse. You may be getting nervous just reading this! But as you'll see in the stories that follow, you are not alone. Find out how others handled wedding-day jitters and still made it to the altar.

THE DETAILS ARE NOW OUT of your hands and there is nothing more you can do but enjoy your day. Try to let the mistakes be a part of the day.

—*ERIN DARWIN*
SAN FRANCISCO, CALIFORNIA

WEDDING DAY JITTERS: THE CHAMPAGNE REALLY DID THE TRICK!

—*TINA COUCH*
FRISCO, TEXAS
NUMBER OF WEDDING GUESTS: 51

HEAD LINES
Best Advice and Top Tips

- Make a checklist to ensure that you don't forget anything on the day of your wedding.

- Ask a trusted friend to be in charge of the wedding-day details and attend to any problems.

- Relax: exercise, take a nap, make a party out of getting dressed for the ceremony.

- A pre-wedding cocktail does wonders for pre-wedding nerves.

- Expect the unexpected: Every detail may not turn out exactly as you hoped, but don't let that ruin your special day.

TAKE THE TIME TO BE "IN THE MOMENT" on your wedding day. I still retain the memory of special moments: seeing my husband at the altar, seeing my grandmother peeking into my room while I sat in front of my mirror and peeked back at her. I remember her face all smiley, and her white hair beautifully adorned with a pink netted hat. Her dress was equally as pink! Memories of a look or a word will remain with us all our lives.

—ANONYMOUS
LONG VALLEY, NEW JERSEY

• • • • • • • •

I WAS BLOWING UP **100** BALLOONS for the reception most of the day of the wedding. It's hard to feel nervous or anxious when you are so light-headed!

—SAMANTHA HIKTOFSEN
GERRY, NEW YORK
NUMBER OF WEDDING GUESTS: 150

PUT A FRIEND IN CHARGE of last-minute details. Just before my wedding, I went into the reception room. To my dismay, it was set up completely differently than expected. Luckily, my friend-in-charge sent me off to finish getting ready, and when I came back just before the ceremony, the room was breathtaking—better than I'd even dared to dream.

—*JODI LAZAR HALL*
SAN FRANCISCO, CALIFORNIA
NUMBER OF WEDDING GUESTS: 100

· · · · · · · ·

"My best man and I spent an hour right before the wedding watching old cartoons. There is nothing that will relax you more than watching *Tom and Jerry* or *The Flintstones.*"

—*JOHN KEVELTY*
WATTS FLATS, NEW YORK
NUMBER OF WEDDING GUESTS: 150

· · · · · · · ·

FOR HIGH-STRESS EVENTS, have a last-minute checklist. My husband-to-be was late to show up at the wedding site. When he finally showed up, he told me that he had gotten to the hotel room and checked in, only to find he had no socks for the wedding! He finally found some with the assistance of the hotel staff.

—*SUSANNE M. ALEXANDER*
CLEVELAND, OHIO

FROM THE EXPERT: ALL WOUND UP

Things get tough in those last weeks, and emotions can run very high. I know: I've seen everything. What I always recommend to our brides is this: In the days leading up to your wedding, take some time to go to a day spa and spend a whole day just chilling out. Get a massage, have a facial, a mud bath—all those exotic treatments—and just pretend you're away somewhere. Leave the wedding on the other side of the door. Try to keep calm. But remember, facials should be scheduled at least three days before your wedding to give your skin time to recover.

A Cincinnati, Ohio, spa called Exclusively Male offers a groom-groomsmen special, including hairstyling, manicure and pedicure, for $90 a person.

MAKE A PARTY OUT OF GETTING YOUR HAIR and nails done on the morning of the wedding. Invite your bridesmaids; go out to the salon together, or get someone to come to your home to do it for all of you. It's a great way to start the day.

—*K.F.*
CANFIELD, OHIO
NUMBER OF WEDDING GUESTS: 100

. . . .

WE HAD OUR WEDDING AT A BEACH HOUSE, and it had three floors. I have an uncle who's in a wheelchair, and I repeatedly told my brother's wife, who was dealing with the caterer, that the food had to be on the first floor so that my uncle could get to it. When I got to the house, where was the food? On the third floor, of course. I could have let that ruin my whole day; I could have turned into Bridezilla. But at that point you've got to take a deep breath and let go.

—*GRACE*
CHAPEL HILL, NORTH CAROLINA

I *RAN* THE NERVOUSNESS OUT OF ME on the morning of my wedding day. I went for a long jog by myself and felt much calmer when I got back. Running always does that for me.

—*SALLY REDMOND*
JAMESTOWN, NEW YORK
NUMBER OF WEDDING GUESTS: 200

ASK A FRIEND TO LOOK OUT for any valuables. This way you don't have to worry about them; a small, but important detail!

—*JODI LAZAR HALL*
SAN FRANCISCO, CALIFORNIA
NUMBER OF WEDDING GUESTS: 100

TO AVOID STRESS—especially the really bad, last-minute-panic kind of stress—think through every detail before your wedding. I thought I had prepared for everything. But on the morning of my wedding when I was at home with the photographer, I suddenly realized that everyone else had left to go to the church, and I didn't have a ride there! I ended up going with the photographer in his MG!

—*ANN SAAVEDRA*
WALNUT CREEK, CALIFORNIA

I SCHEDULED A BREAKFAST DATE with my mom on the morning of the wedding. She has such a great sense of humor that I knew she'd be able to loosen me up. We had a nice time. We talked about when I was little, and she told me what to expect at the wedding and afterward. I felt much more relaxed after breakfast than I would have if I had been sitting at home all day watching the clock tick.

—*RACHAEL JACKSON*
DRY RIDGE, KENTUCKY
NUMBER OF WEDDING GUESTS: 160

I ate a whole bag of gold-fish crackers and spent the entire day with my bridal party.

—*LACEY YANTIS*
BLANK
BOTHELL,
WASHINGTON
NUMBER OF WEDDING GUESTS: 120

GROOMS: READ THIS!

SEND YOUR WIFE-TO-BE A DOZEN RED ROSES on your wedding day. Have them delivered to her house first thing in the morning. She will be thrilled. I did it, and I have sent my wife the same roses on the morning of each of our anniversaries.

—JOHN ATWORTH
HUBBARD, OHIO
NUMBER OF WEDDING GUESTS: 200

IF YOU HAVE YOUR BUDDIES UP TO YOUR WEDDING SUITE to get ready for the wedding, make sure you call housekeeping before you leave so that the room will be clean when you bring your new wife back after the reception.

—JOSH
ST. PETERSBURG, FLORIDA
NUMBER OF WEDDING GUESTS: 250

CALL YOUR BRIDE-TO-BE. Tell her a funny joke. Ask her to tell you a joke. My wife and I were hardly ever apart; knowing that I couldn't see her before the wedding contributed to making me jittery. But we found that although we couldn't see each other we could talk on the phone all we wanted. I really think we were able to calm each other down through our phone calls. Just hearing her voice calmed me.

—LONNIE PRETNOS
CAMPBELL, OHIO
NUMBER OF WEDDING GUESTS: 50

I TOOK A NAP IN THE EARLY AFTERNOON of my wedding day. I didn't sleep half the time, but just lying down in a bed tends to make you relax. Plus, you need to conserve your energy for the late night ahead.

—J.A.
ATLANTA, GEORGIA
NUMBER OF WEDDING GUESTS: 200

. . . .

" Use a low-grade sedative to take the edge off. Mine were my "something old," because it was actually my grandmother's sedative. Some people take a grandmother's handkerchief, some people take their grandmother's jewelry. I got Grandma's Valium: worked like a charm. "

—D.S.
BROOKLYN, NEW YORK
NUMBER OF WEDDING GUESTS: 150

. . . .

GET SOME XANAX! The morning of my wedding, I was sitting in the beauty salon with my bridesmaids, and the panic set in. I simply said, "Someone get me some Xanax. Otherwise, I'm not sure I'm going to make it to the wedding!"

—BECKY GREENSPAN SLEMONS
SAVANNAH, GEORGIA
NUMBER OF WEDDING GUESTS: 150

STAY CALM ON YOUR WEDDING DAY. Little things are bound to go wrong, but usually there's not much you can do about it. On our wedding day the florist only brought enough boutonnieres for half of the groomsmen and none for the fathers of the bride and groom. Instead of freaking out, we just pulled from the boutonnieres we had to make enough for everyone and nobody noticed the difference.

—MICHELE
ATLANTA, GEORGIA
NUMBER OF WEDDING GUESTS: 200

There is only one foolproof way to get rid of jitters, my friends: tequila, tequila, and more tequila.

—J.D.
WATTS FLATS,
NEW YORK
NUMBER OF WED-
DING GUESTS: 100

· · · · · · · · ·

EVEN IF YOU AND YOUR SOON-TO-BE spouse are perfectly matched, you are bound to feel some anxiety; getting married is such a huge, life-altering experience. My hands were shaking terribly during my wedding ceremony, so much so that you could see the bouquet shaking on the videotape, but that didn't stop me from going through with it. I just accepted the fact that I was going to feel nervous, and that nervousness was one of many feelings (including excitement and enormous joy) that I would be experiencing throughout the day.

—RACHEL GREENE BALDINO
SHREWSBURY, MASSACHUSETTS

· · · · · · · · ·

DON'T LET YOURSELF BE A BRIDEZILLA on your wedding day. Stop all your last-minute preparations at noon on the day before your wedding. Leave the work to others. From that moment on, relax. Go to a spa, get your hair done, polish your nails. Accept that you've done your best and whatever else happens is out of your hands.

—TEENA GOMEZ
CORONA, CALIFORNIA

THE SILVER LINING …

Expect the unexpected, but don't let it get you stressed. The morning of my wedding, I woke to the sound of rain drumming against my window. It poured the rest of the day—so much so that major highways were closed due to flooding. When I left my hairdresser's that morning, I had to wear a garbage bag over my head, or my hair and veil would have been ruined! At first, I was really stressed: I couldn't believe it was pouring on my wedding day! But everyone arrived safely, which was the most important thing, and the wedding went on! The best part? The rain let up just as the ceremony finished, and we were able to get a photo outside that became my favorite one from the whole day. In that photo, my white dress almost glows against the black sky. I guess there's always a silver lining.

—A.K.
ALBURTIS, PENNSYLVANIA

YOU HEAR SO MANY HORROR STORIES about people forgetting to bring stuff to the church or the reception or having to make last-minute changes. We decided to designate one of my cousins to be  on standby for any last-minute running around that needed doing. And we did need him: I broke a shoelace on my rental shoes and he had to run to the store for me. And my wife left for the church without her earrings and he had to run back to her mother's house to get them. It's nice to be prepared for the unexpected, if you can.

—J.C.
DRY RIDGE, KENTUCKY
NUMBER OF WEDDING GUESTS: 150

Wear sun block if you go golfing before the wedding.

—JOSH
ST. PETERSBURG, FLORIDA
NUMBER OF WEDDING GUESTS: 250

TO SEE, OR NOT TO SEE?

I DON'T BELIEVE THAT IT'S BAD LUCK for the bride and groom to see each other before the ceremony. In fact, we hung out together for most of the day. He's a hairstylist; he even did my hair! I think it helped to keep us from being so nervous.

> —A.H.
> *OZARK, MISSOURI*
> *NUMBER OF WEDDING GUESTS: 150*

I ADVISE YOU NOT ONLY TO NOT SEE YOUR BRIDE, but don't see anyone in her bridal party. My wife was freaking out before the wedding, and I never would have known if I hadn't caught her maid of honor in the hall looking like she was scared to go back to the bride. I'll never forget the look on that poor girl's face. I was convinced, right up until my wife walked down the aisle, that she was going to bail; that she had changed her mind and was having a breakdown. Turns out she wasn't happy with her hair or something, but the maid of honor wouldn't even tell me what the problem was. She thought if she did she'd get in trouble. Stay on opposite sides of town until the actual moment.

> —*CHRIS*
> *CHAPEL HILL, NORTH CAROLINA*
> *NUMBER OF WEDDING GUESTS: 230*

SEE EACH OTHER BEFORE THE CEREMONY. I know it's nontraditional. Make it a "big" entrance and have your photographer and videographer capture the moment your husband first sees you in your beautiful gown. Then you can take all of your traditional pictures. And then you can enjoy the cocktail hour with your family and friends, rather than taking pictures.

> —*JESSICA CARLIN*
> *NEW YORK, NEW YORK*
> *NUMBER OF WEDDING GUESTS: 150*

THE BEGINNING OF MY WEDDING was stressful for me! It took me a while to unwind. There was another wedding ending, and I overlapped a little with the other party. I'd advise the bride and groom to wait until the last possible minute to arrive at the venue, so you don't get stressed about what's happening there (leave last-minute logistics to others!).

—*ANONYMOUS*
TORONTO, ONTARIO, CANADA
NUMBER OF WEDDING GUESTS: 175

. . . .

"The morning of our wedding, I peeked out the window to see my fiancé washing his car! I think it was very therapeutic for him. "

—*TARA GREEN*
ATLANTA, GEORGIA
NUMBER OF WEDDING GUESTS: 120

. . . .

IT'S ALMOST IMPOSSIBLE TO REMEMBER TO EAT, but I'm telling you, it's critical! Appoint one of your bridesmaids, or little sisters, or nephews, or whomever, to bring you some food every once in a while. Don't have them ask you what you want, because you will inevitably be too distracted to care or answer. Just tell them in advance to bring you some simple toast, sandwiches, fruit, yogurt—things that are easy to eat without getting sick or ruining makeup and clothes.

—*JEN W.*
SAN CARLOS, CALIFORNIA

FROM THE EXPERT:
BRIDAL ILLUSION

I caught up to one of the most beautiful brides I'd ever worked with after her ceremony, at the cocktail hour. There she was, drinking a *beer*. Looking so magnificent, and drinking *beer* from a *bottle*. And I said, "Jesus Christ, Jessica!" I took the beer, got a champagne glass, and poured the beer into the champagne glass.

Ladies, that dress cost a fortune. Don't ruin the illusion.

DON'T LET THE LITTLE THINGS BOTHER YOU. For my wedding, everyone was supposed to wear white shoes. Right before the ceremony, when I was having pictures taken at my mother's house, I looked down and saw one of my bridesmaids had on gold shoes. I wanted to scream. But weird stuff is bound to happen and it doesn't matter in the end.

—*L.A.*
STRATFORD, CONNECTICUT
NUMBER OF WEDDING GUESTS: 100

• • • • • • • • •

WORRIED ABOUT WEDDING-DAY JITTERS? Think of something funny; something that always makes you laugh. It could be a joke, a scene from a movie, or something your fiancé does that cracks you up! Keep that "funny" on hand and in mind when you get nervous. It should lighten your mood and your mind when those wedding-day jitters come around.

—*JENNIFER BRISMAN*
NEW YORK, NEW YORK
NUMBER OF WEDDING GUESTS: 200

Saying "I Do": Surviving (and Enjoying) the Ceremony

I n the United States, there are over two million weddings every year; over 6,000 per day. This is our way of telling you that, yes, you will survive it, as millions do every year. But as you prepare to take your vows with the love of your life, you probably feel like the one-in-two-million who won't make it through the process. How do you keep from fainting? How do you enjoy the moment? From those who traveled down the aisle and back up again, here's advice on how to avoid stumbling on the way.

AS YOU GET READY to walk down the aisle, stand tall, breathe deeply, and calm down. Walk very slowly. You can't walk too slowly; you want to give everyone the opportunity to see you.

—ANN SAAVEDRA
WALNUT CREEK, CALIFORNIA

YOU CAN DO IT! JUST TAKE A DEEP BREATH. YOU'RE ABOUT TO HAVE THE BEST TIME OF YOUR LIFE.

—MICHELE
ATLANTA, GEORGIA
NUMBER OF WEDDING
GUESTS: 200

HEAD LINES
Best Advice and Top Tips

- Enjoy the walk down the aisle and take your time—before you know it, the whole day will be a memory.

- Talk to your spouse beforehand about the kiss—do you want it to be short and sweet, or long and passionate?

- Things may go wrong during the ceremony, so keep a sense of humor.

- Right after the ceremony, take some time to spend alone with your new spouse.

I REMEMBER COMING DOWN THE AISLE with my mom and dad and seeing my husband standing there with tears in his eyes. My husband and I had dated for about five years before we got married and I never knew him to be a very emotional person. When I saw those tears in his eyes, I felt I was getting a glimpse of how much he loved me. Enjoy those little moments!

—JILL
IRVING, TEXAS
NUMBER OF WEDDING GUESTS: 100

• • • • • • • •

FOR A WHILE I WAS THINKING that I totally knew why people eloped and that maybe it wouldn't have been all that bad if we had. But now that the big day has come and gone, I am so glad we did it the way we did. It was awesome.

—D.S.
DURHAM, NORTH CAROLINA
NUMBER OF WEDDING GUESTS: 175

FROM THE EXPERT: MARCHING MUSIC

There are wonderful, standard choices for processional music—Bach's *Air on the G String*, *Arioso*, or Pachelbel's *Canon*—but many couples like to get away from the standards, to personalize their ceremonies. They look for music that really means something to them.

A lot of our brides are walking down to "O" from Cirque du Soleil; or to their favorite rock music. We had a 14-piece orchestra at one wedding, and the bride chose a Pink Floyd number for one of the members of her bridal party to walk down the aisle to. I almost dropped dead, but it sounded great.

For the flower girls and ring bearers, we like "Rainbow Connection," or the feather theme from *Forrest Gump*.

MY HUSBAND AND I TOOK A LOT OF TIME planning the ceremony itself to make it really reflect our love for each other. We worked with the pastor and wrote the entire service, including our own vows. We chose special music that was performed by close friends, had a candlelight service, and set aside time within the service to acknowledge our parents and their roles in our lives. It was a very emotional service that brought even the most stoic guest to tears. To this day, people who attended our wedding say it was the most beautiful and memorable wedding ceremony they ever attended.

> —DEANNA
> MACUNGIE, PENNSYLVANIA

FROM THE EXPERT: A HELPING HAND

It's happened more than once that I have had to encourage a bride to take that first step down the aisle.

One bride absolutely adored her husband-to-be, but she froze. I gave her a gentle push and said, "Just do it." She did it.

Another one had already had a baby with her fiancé; the baby had just been carried down the aisle, and now she was shaking; she had a case of the jitters. I said, "You have got to do this. You already had his kid, you want to marry him, and *that's it.*" That was it.

THE MOST MAGICAL MOMENT FOR ME was walking down the stairs (about to go down a long aisle!) and seeing my future husband's eyes and all the people I love the most looking back at me. I felt an immense amount of love in the room and it was a feeling I don't think I had had before.

—*JENIFER MANN*
CASTRO VALLEY, CALIFORNIA
NUMBER OF WEDDING GUESTS: 35

• • • • • • • •

IT IS ALWAYS SO TOUCHING TO SEE a bride and groom stop after the ceremony and hug their parents and grandparents on the way out of the church. My oldest son and his wife stopped to give us hugs and a rose. It is an open acknowledgement of the mutual love and respect the bride and groom and their parents have for each other.

—*CLAUDIA*
SAN ANTONIO, TEXAS
NUMBER OF WEDDING GUESTS: 250

WE TALKED ABOUT THE KISS before the ceremony and agreed that we would keep it short because we didn't want to offend anyone. But it didn't turn out the way I expected. I was shocked when my husband grabbed me and gave me this long, passionate kiss.

—*JULIE FOCKLER*
LEE'S SUMMIT, MISSOURI
NUMBER OF WEDDING GUESTS: 200

" If I could change one thing: I would have walked down the aisle twice as slow as I did. You plan for months and then the whole day is over in the blink of an eye. I would have walked down that aisle at a snail's pace so that I could take it all in and savor every moment. "

—*CYNTHIA CLARKE*
INDEPENDENCE, KENTUCKY

WHAT'S THE WORST THAT COULD HAPPEN?

WHO WOULD HAVE THOUGHT that my husband's 91-year-old great-grandmother would come to the wedding, fall down a flight of stairs, and have to go to the emergency room just 45 minutes before the ceremony started? Fortunately, two of my bridesmaids had medical training and were able to help. Great-Grandma was even able to make it to the reception a few hours later!

> —M.H.
> RICHMOND, INDIANA
> NUMBER OF WEDDING GUESTS: 265

OUR WEDDING CAKE DID NOT SHOW UP. When my parents called to see where it was, the cake lady told them that she thought the wedding was the following week! Fortunately, the bakery supplied a couple of sheet cakes and a fake one for pictures. My husband didn't tell me there was anything wrong until the problem was taken care of and we were at the reception: nice guy!

> —CRYSTAL SMITH
> DUBOIS, PENNSYLVANIA

AT ONE WEDDING I WENT TO—LUCKILY NOT MY OWN!—the rabbi spilled red wine down the bride's dress during the ceremony. That meant she had a stained dress for the rest of the ceremony and the entire reception. He tried to make the best of it by making up some story about how that was good luck of some sort. But basically, he just ruined her dress and her wedding photos.

> —S.F.
> SAN FRANCISCO, CALIFORNIA
> NUMBER OF WEDDING GUESTS: 150

A HALF-HOUR BEFORE THE CEREMONY, my mother-in-law accidentally cut my bouquet to spice up the centerpieces. My friend stopped her and told her it was mine, at which point, my poor mother-in-law started to cry!

> *—ANONYMOUS*
> *TORONTO, ONTARIO, CANADA*
> *NUMBER OF WEDDING GUESTS: 175*

THERE WAS A HORRIBLE TRAFFIC JAM in the city that day and even though we spent time and money on shuttle services, it took guests over two hours to get to the wedding, instead of the 45 minutes it should have taken. Some of my out-of-town guests actually missed my ceremony.

> *—KALYNA*
> *SAN FRANCISCO, CALIFORNIA*
> *NUMBER OF WEDDING GUESTS: 120*

AT THE CONCLUSION, THE OFFICIANT SAID, "I now pronounce you husband and wife, Mr. and Mrs. Aaron Yantis." My last name is actually Blank. Needless to say, I will never live that one down—my friends and family still call me Mr. Yantis.

> *—AARON BLANK*
> *SEATTLE, WASHINGTON*
> *NUMBER OF WEDDING GUESTS: 125*

IF YOU'RE PLANNING A WEDDING ANYWHERE it might snow, don't think you're safe with a fall or spring wedding! We had ours in April and got walloped with a late-season snowstorm, which meant some of our guests' flights were cancelled and others couldn't drive in. I hope there's no next time, but if there is, I'm going for summer!

> *—J.W.*
> *ROCHESTER, NEW YORK*

ALL EYES (AND CAMERAS, AND MICS) ON YOU

DURING MY WEDDING I HAD THE WORST CASE of cotton-mouth. I knew the kiss was coming up so I thought I would take care of the situation. During the prayer I figured I had my back to the guests and the pastor had his eyes closed, so I tried to work up some saliva in my mouth by rolling my tongue around and around in big circles. The kiss came and all was good. When I arrived home from my honeymoon I was greeted at the airport by my family. When I asked if they had the wedding tape, they all started laughing. I could not figure out what was so funny. Finally, my dad told me that the video camera was right behind the pastor and caught the whole episode and me "working up some spit" up close. When I saw the video I was horrified. I looked like a cow chewing gum. The videos had already been sent to some relatives so I knew my secret was out.

— *TIFFANY*
OKLAHOMA CITY, OKLAHOMA
NUMBER OF WEDDING GUESTS: 40-50

• • • • • • • •

MAKE SURE THAT YOU ARE AWARE OF *ALL* MICROPHONES that will be near you during the ceremony. My fiancé was wearing two microphones, one on each lapel. I was under the impression that he was only wearing one on the right side. After the vows, the minister announced, "You may kiss the bride." I leaned in for my first kiss as a married woman. After the kiss, I gave a heavy sigh of relief that the ceremony was over—right into the microphone. It echoed throughout the room, sounding more like a moan of passion than a sigh of relief. Eight years later, I still hear about it at dinner parties.

— *SHELLY BEAUMONT*
GRANDVIEW, TEXAS
NUMBER OF WEDDING GUESTS: 450

MY FAVORITE PART OF THE WEDDING was the first time my soon-to-be husband saw me as a bride. The look on his face was just priceless; I'll never forget it.

—*SIMONE*
  THORNHILL, ONTARIO, CANADA
  NUMBER OF WEDDING GUESTS: 250

" My fiancé had written "Help Me" on the bottom of his shoes. So when we knelt down in church, everybody started cracking up and I couldn't figure out why. I didn't get upset when I found out; I cracked up, too. "

—*ANONYMOUS*
  ETOWAH, NORTH CAROLINA

THE HARDEST THING TO DO on your wedding day is also the most important: You have to make time stop. You have to take the time in the midst of all the craziness to realize what is happening and just enjoy it. It will be the shortest day of your life. If you blink, it's over. Try to live in the moment as much as you can. Don't rush through it. Take time to talk to people and hug people and cry with people. On the day you die, this is the day that will have the most clarity in your memory.

—*MARCIA COULIS*
  BOARDMAN, OHIO
  NUMBER OF WEDDING GUESTS: 100

SECOND TIME'S A CHARM

DO IT THE WAY YOU WANTED IT THE FIRST TIME. Go with your instinct. I had more control over the wedding the second time: it was smaller. And the rock on my finger was bigger: it went up a carat and a half.

> —*ANONYMOUS*
> *NEW YORK, NEW YORK*

• • • • • • • •

BECAUSE THIS WAS A SECOND wedding for both of us, we made all our plans together. It was fun to be creative and still plan a meaningful ceremony and day for us.

> —*DAWN WINBLAD*
> *INDIANAPOLIS, INDIANA*
> *NUMBER OF WEDDING GUESTS: 30*

• • • • • • • •

SECOND WEDDINGS ARE AN ANTICLIMAX: You've been there, he's been there, and a lot of people at your wedding have been there with you. We didn't need to make a social statement or spend money. We didn't need presents to validate the union. I had 100 people in my house. We did almost all the cooking. I wanted this to be an extension of our home, of our love, of our circle. I didn't invite work friends, I didn't have distant relatives; I only had the people I wanted to be with me and wish me well.

> —*A.P.*
> *PHILADELPHIA, PENNSYLVANIA*
> *NUMBER OF WEDDING GUESTS: 100*

• • • • • • • •

I SAY YOU CAN WEAR WHITE if you want to; the days of the Inquisition are over. If I can't wear white after my first wedding, what's next? Wear white, wear pink, wear thong underwear and show it to the crowd if you want. Who makes up these rules, anyway?

> —*HALLIE UMBERT*
> *DRY RIDGE, KENTUCKY*
> *NUMBER OF WEDDING GUESTS: 125*

PEOPLE SAY SECOND MARRIAGES SHOULD BE SMALLER and less of a big deal. But I'm not so sure I agree. That's almost like giving up before you start, unless you just didn't have fun the first time. But my first wedding was great, and I thought of it very fondly, even if the marriage itself wasn't so great. I was happy for an excuse to do it all again—have the big party, wear the tux, pretend that it was the first time. I'm glad we did that; I'm glad that the first wedding I had doesn't outshine the second in my memory.

—*CHRIS*
CHAPEL HILL, NORTH CAROLINA
NUMBER OF WEDDING GUESTS: 230

I PREFERRED MY SECOND, SMALLER WEDDING, with only 40 invited guests as opposed to more than 200 for the first. The big wedding was so stressful, cost so much, and took so long to plan. On top of that, there was so much going on, it was just a blur. At the small second wedding, there was no stress. We threw it together in three weeks, and it cost far less than the first one. It was just like having a party with many dear friends, and in the middle of it we got married.

—*PATRICIA*
COZUMEL, MEXICO
NUMBER OF WEDDING GUESTS: 40

WHEN GEORGE AND I WERE MARRIED, I was a divorcée and he was a widower, so we had both been through it before. This time, we really wanted it to be about us, not about the show, or the flowers, or the money we spent. We had just a few people, spent almost no money, and it was lovely! George's daughter picked flowers from her garden, we had a small party afterward, and we saved our money for the honeymoon, which is supposed to be the best part anyway.

—*BETTY*
DURHAM, NORTH CAROLINA
NUMBER OF WEDDING GUESTS: 15

THE MOMENT THE STONE CHAPEL'S double doors opened, revealing me to the congregation, all I saw was my soon-to-be husband. His face is the only one I remember from my walk down the aisle. I recall him sucking in a breath. He says I took his breath away. It still makes me smile.

—*TRESA MCBEE*
SPRINGFIELD, MISSOURI

• • • • • • • •

" Bring a small, discreet pack of mints up to the altar with you—not just for yourself, but for your soon-to-be-hubby, and also for the priest. Nerves give you bad breath, so all three of you will likely need them. "

—*MARIE LONG*
HARRISONBURG, VIRGINIA
NUMBER OF WEDDING GUESTS: 200

• • • • • • • •

MAKE SURE YOU ARE CLOSE to a restroom before the ceremony. My petticoat and bra were sewn into my dress. I swear I jumped completely out of my dress in nothing but pantyhose 15 times to run to the restroom before I headed down the aisle.

—*SHELLY BEAUMONT*
GRANDVIEW, TEXAS
NUMBER OF WEDDING GUESTS: 450

FROM THE EXPERT: DOGS AND OTHER SIGNIFICANT OTHERS

The wedding was at a Palm Beach hotel, and the couple wanted their dog in the ceremony. The dog was their baby, but the hotel didn't see it that way; dogs were not allowed, period. We brought the dog into the hotel in a carrying case. Just before the ceremony began, we took him out of the case and he walked down the aisle with the nephews. He was wearing a black bow tie, and he sat for the entire ceremony, then left. It was the cutest thing you ever saw in your life.

I have no hesitation about including dogs in the ceremony. It has worked out very well, in my experience. It's almost as if the pets understand the joyousness of the occasion.

On the other hand, a bride with a wedding at an exclusive club wanted to have her parrot be part of the ceremony. She really insisted upon it. *She wanted her parrot.* The bird flew up onto one of the carved elephants and just perched there. We're lucky it didn't do its business on the carpet.

Other than well-trained dogs, pets attending your wedding is not something I recommend.

IT WAS PRETTY AMAZING TO HAVE EVERYONE I loved at my wedding. I looked out at the audience—my friends and family—and I was in awe. I don't know that that'll happen ever again, so I cherished that part of my wedding.

—*HEATHER GLOVER*
NEW YORK, NEW YORK

• • • • • • • •

WITH THE KISS, I say go for it. When are you going to have the chance again to have 200 people watching you make out?

—*MATT MARSHALL*
EVANS CITY, PENNSYLVANIA
NUMBER OF WEDDING GUESTS: 250

• • • • • • • •

DURING OUR CEREMONY, my husband and I gave each of our moms a single-stem rose to thank them for helping so much.

—*ABBY SCALF*
ROUND LAKE BEACH, ILLINOIS

• • • • • • • •

I'M RARELY SPEECHLESS, but I was so amazed when I first saw my wife in her wedding dress that I couldn't speak!

—*MITCH*
TORONTO, ONTARIO, CANADA
NUMBER OF WEDDING GUESTS: 200

Party Time: Your Reception

*Y*ou're married! Now comes the fun part—your time to let loose and celebrate with all your friends. And family. And family you've never met. And friends of friends you've never met. From the first dance to the speeches to the relatives you don't know how to talk to, there's a lot to consider. There's also a script to follow. Here's how to make everyone happy while having the time of your life.

THERE'S A TRADITION at a Jewish wedding reception in which the bride and groom are lifted up on chairs. I've never experienced anything like that; it was so much fun! I literally felt like I was flying!

—*SHIRA GREEN*
TORONTO, ONTARIO, CANADA
NUMBER OF WEDDING GUESTS: 220

I LOVED THE SPEECHES. THEY WERE SO TOUCHING!

—*ANONYMOUS*
TORONTO, ONTARIO, CANADA
NUMBER OF WEDDING GUESTS: 175

FROM THE EXPERT: GUEST FAVORS

Guest favors have evolved into a necessary and expected gesture in the past decade. Here's my favorite gift for guests: Magnificent chocolates in an oval box, covered in moiré fabric matching the reception's color scheme, and tied beautifully with a bow. Inside, under the cover, is a little note that says thank you for joining us, we hope you had as good a time as we did, sweet dreams. It's signed by the couple. The note is a nice touch.

If everyone is speaking to each other at the end of the wedding, then you can consider it a success!

—ANONYMOUS
TORONTO,
ONTARIO, CANADA
NUMBER OF WED-
DING GUESTS: 145

MAKE SURE TO INCLUDE some cultural elements from both the husband and wife, especially if there are different religions, cultures, nationalities. We had Filipino appetizers and lots of Filipino traditions mixed in for my husband and his family, even though it was primarily an American-style wedding.

—JULIE
SAN FRANCISCO, CALIFORNIA

• • • • • • • • •

ONE OF THE COOLEST THINGS at the reception was the way the guys in my wedding party took care of me. They wouldn't let me go up to get a drink or food or anything. They brought everything to me. I have never been pampered like that in my life. The first time I tried to get up from the table, my best man asked me where I was going. I told him I wanted a beer. He said it would be taken care of. He told me that except for trips to the bathroom, everything else would be handled for me.

—JOSH GRANSON
MELROSE, VIRGINIA
NUMBER OF WEDDING GUESTS: 200

WE HAD A DANCE FEATURING THE OLDEST and youngest guests. It ended up being my grandfather, who was 85, and my niece, who was 18 months. He was actually in a wheelchair at the time and he kind of held her on his lap and spun her around a little during the song.

> —*KIM SWIATEK*
> *WATTS FLATS, NEW YORK*
> *NUMBER OF WEDDING GUESTS: 200*

. . . .

66 While we were cutting the cake I managed to slice my husband's thumb with the knife. It was really his fault for getting his thumb in the way. It was more embarrassing than anything else, but it's something he still teases me about from time to time. 99

> —*SALLY REDMOND*
> *JAMESTOWN, NEW YORK*
> *NUMBER OF WEDDING GUESTS: 200*

. . . .

WE HAD TOO MANY SPEECHES! We scheduled two speeches before dinner and four after dinner. Less is more. If I did it again, I would take two of the assigned speech people and make them our MCs, so that their speeches could be incorporated throughout the night.

> —*ANONYMOUS*
> *TORONTO, ONTARIO, CANADA*
> *NUMBER OF WEDDING GUESTS: 175*

A TOAST! (WHO GOES FIRST?)

A traditional order of toasts at a wedding reception:

1. Best Man
2. Fathers (groom's, then bride's)
3. Groom
4. Bride
5. Friends and Relatives
6. Maid/Matron of Honor
7. Mothers (groom's, then bride's)
8. Open the floor

WE SERVED A COLD, RED FRUIT SOUP as the first course and my wedding veil went into the soup! I wanted to keep my veil on (didn't like my hair that day!) but I also was terrified that the red on the veil would quickly drip down and stain my white dress. A server quickly noticed the situation and ran over to help me. She grabbed the veil away from my dress and washed it off in the kitchen. Whew!

—*SHIRA GREEN*
TORONTO, ONTARIO, CANADA
NUMBER OF WEDDING GUESTS: 220 GUESTS

• • • • • • • • •

WE ALWAYS GO TO A PARTY TOGETHER but talk to different people all night. We decided beforehand to tag-team everything: We stuck together for most of the night, and if more than 10 minutes had gone by we stopped what we were doing and found each other. Also, it was really fun to say, "Excuse me, I need to find my *husband*."

—*D.S.*
DURHAM, NORTH CAROLINA
NUMBER OF WEDDING GUESTS: 165

DEALING WITH ALL THE PEOPLE

MEETING AND GREETING PEOPLE YOU'VE NEVER MET: The key is to make it seem like you are long-lost friends. It's your job to make everyone feel more than welcome. You should make them feel like you couldn't have had the wedding without them. People will remember the way you greet them at your wedding. I had a few distant relatives whom I hardly ever had contact with before my wedding. But after I had treated them well they would send anniversary and Christmas cards each year.

> —*DONNA ROWE*
> *FRANKFORT, KENTUCKY*

HAVE A STORY READY TO TELL the great aunts and obscure relatives that will make them think they have the inside scoop on the wedding.

> —*EVAN*
> *ATLANTA, GEORGIA*
> *NUMBER OF WEDDING GUESTS: 110*

MY MOTHER TOLD ME, JUST MAKE SURE YOU SPEND a couple of minutes with everyone. Once I had done that, the night was over. People have made an effort to be there and bought you something nice; the least you can do is make the effort to spend a few minutes and thank them face-to-face.

> —*AMY*
> *GREENSBORO, NORTH CAROLINA*
> *NUMBER OF WEDDING GUESTS: 120*

DEALING WITH FAMILY: Help mitigate or minimize any social awkwardness by introducing everybody's people to one another and provide a few scraps of potential conversation.

> —*ANONYMOUS*
> *BLUEFIELD, WEST VIRGINIA*
> *NUMBER OF WEDDING GUESTS: 175*

DON'T BE AFRAID TO ASK PEOPLE to get you things and do things for you during the reception. Most people understand that your time is very short that day, and they feel like insiders when they help you out—picking up the bride's car from a parking lot, getting you a plate of food or a drink, putting the gifts in a car, etc.

—EVAN
ATLANTA, GEORGIA
NUMBER OF WEDDING GUESTS: 110

WE HAD SUCH AN AMAZING PARTY: We had a DJ that I knew from University who played what we wanted. It was mid-February so everyone came ready to party. We were all bored and tired of winter and wanted a reason to dress up. We also did it on a Saturday night (early sundown in winter), so no one left.

—MICHELLE ROTHSTEIN
TORONTO, ONTARIO, CANADA
NUMBER OF WEDDING GUESTS: 180

PICTURE THIS

A picture says a thousand words, so why not have a few speak volumes at your wedding? Here are some ideas on how to use old pictures to start conversations and show guests the moments that led up to this big day.

- Print childhood photos of the bride and groom and place them near the cake. With particularly funny or endearing photos, place copies on the tables where people will be seated. This could help spark conversation between family and friends.
- Make a photo family tree to display at your reception. Place in a high-profile place, such as near the guest book.
- In a high-profile spot, feature marriage photos of the couple's parents, grandparents, great-grandparents, and beyond.

GOOD DOG, BAD DOG

DO NOT TAKE YOUR DOG TO YOUR WEDDING RECEPTION. We feel as if our dog is part of the family so we wanted him to be a part of our big day. But it just ended up adding one more problem to a day where you want as few headaches as possible. The dog is usually well behaved, but on that day, when he wasn't getting underfoot he was spending his time begging for food. If I had to do it over I'd leave him at home and bring him a doggy bag.

—*PATRICIA EGTASHTER*
DRY RIDGE, KENTUCKY
NUMBER OF WEDDING GUESTS: 100

• • • • • • • • •

WE REALLY WANTED OUR DOGS IN THE WEDDING CEREMONY. And everyone told us that was a terrible idea, because our dogs are a little crazy. But I wanted them in the pictures, and now I'm really upset that I don't have that.

—*JIM*
RALEIGH, NORTH CAROLINA

SENIOR GUESTS

IF YOU ARE LUCKY ENOUGH TO HAVE GRANDPARENTS, be sure that they don't get lost in the shuffle. Many seniors need to use the bathroom often; get dressed in slow motion—particularly when they are donning unfamiliar, new duds—and can become disoriented in new, crowded surroundings. Allow them the time they need so they can enjoy the day. If necessary, ask a younger friend or relative to be a discreet "grandparent-watcher." These designated individuals can take grandma along when they go to the bathroom—half an hour *before* the ceremony—and ensure that grandpa is in the right place at the right time for dancing and pictures.

> —*CHERYL K.*
> *BROOKLYN, NEW YORK*

• • • • • • • • •

WHEN YOU ARE DEALING WITH OLDER PEOPLE AT THE RECEPTION, you have to speak the language that they speak. More often than not, that is the language of physical contact. Older people like to touch and squeeze and hug and hold you while they talk.

So I beat them to the punch: When I'd approach the table I'd just put my arm around them and give them a squeeze like we were old pals. I really don't think it mattered what I said after that. All that they'd remember was that I treated them like family.

> —*W.T.*
> *HARRISONBURG, VIRGINIA*
> *NUMBER OF WEDDING GUESTS: 75*

TOAST DON'TS

Unless you want to act like someone in a beer commercial, try to refrain from doing the following:

- Joke at the expense of others
- Speak for more than a couple minutes
- Steal the spotlight
- Tell inappropriate stories or use vulgar language
- Drink too much before giving the toast
- Chew gum
- Talk fast

YOU CAN'T JUST SIT THERE and let people get out of hand. I had a friend who didn't know when to quit and started getting ridiculously out of hand. He was going out on the dance floor and pinching girls' butts. I told the bartender to cut him off. The next time he went to get a drink and was refused he came to me to complain. I told him some lie about liability with the hotel. He bought it. That's one good thing about dealing with drunks: You can tell them just about anything.

—*BENNY LAPORTE*
FRANKFORT, KENTUCKY
NUMBER OF WEDDING GUESTS: 125

• • • • • • • • •

DON'T SHOVE CAKE IN EACH OTHER'S FACES. It's not a funny, spontaneous moment anymore; it's been done to death. And believe me, most women don't want cake all over their faces and in their hair. I sure didn't! Just feed each other the cake as delicately as possible and get on with the party.

—*N.C.*
HOUSTON, TEXAS

FROM THE EXPERT:
GONE WITH THE WIND

Here are some wedding-reception rituals that seem to have fallen into disuse:

Receiving lines: Most people don't have them. You'd end up spending half the reception standing by the door. It ties up the wedding party *and* the guests—they can't get into the party.

Instead of a receiving line, be diligent about saying hello to every guest individually. It's the nice thing for both the bride and the groom to do.

Garter removal/bouquet tossing: This questionable practice is nearly extinct. Even bouquet throwing is on the wane. These days, it is mostly young brides who still make this tradition a part of their wedding. Most brides like to keep their bouquets, and who can blame them?

MY FATHER-IN-LAW LIKES TO TELL DIRTY JOKES, and he told one in his speech. It was a very interesting welcome into the family; I don't like to relive it. I've blocked that out. Make sure you know what people are going to say before you give them the mic; especially if your boss is there.

—ANONYMOUS
NEW YORK, NEW YORK

• • • • • • • •

AT THE RECEPTION WE HAD A TABLE set out with challah so that my grandfather could recite the blessing, and then we could all break bread together and eat, which is a Jewish tradition. Well, I married a Catholic guy, and the Catholic side of the guest list wandered by the table and must have thought, "Yum, bread!" They ate it all before we could even begin. If you are going to do things that are part of a tradition for one side but completely new to the other side, make sure you explain beforehand or at least put out a "Do not touch" sign!

—LISA NASEEF
CAPE ELIZABETH, MAINE
NUMBER OF WEDDING GUESTS: 120

• • • • • • • •

ONE THING I WISH I COULD CHANGE about our wedding video is the part near the end where the video guy asked people to say a kind word or two to me and my husband. The problem is that he did it at the end of the reception. So we have 35 minutes of our family and friends stumbling around drunk and slurring their words. He shouldn't have done it when he saw the condition some of those people were in. If you are going to do that kind of thing, tell your video guy to do it early in the evening.

—ANONYMOUS
FLORENCE, KENTUCKY
NUMBER OF WEDDING GUESTS: 150

Make arrangements for leaving the reception. We didn't, and we were left at the hall. My parents had to give us a ride to the hotel!

—C.V.
SHELTON, CONNECTICUT
NUMBER OF WEDDING GUESTS: 100

HEAD LINES
Best Advice and Top Tips

- Spend your wedding night in a hotel instead of your family home. You don't want to hear your relatives talking and laughing through the floor on your first night together as husband and wife.

- Be prepared for the fact that you both may be too exhausted on your wedding night to actually have sex.

- If you want your wedding night to be romantic, plan it ahead of time: champagne, rose petals, a private room.

- Give yourself a couple of days before you leave for your honeymoon—it will give you some extra time to spend celebrating with your family, and allow you to leave for your trip well-rested.

- When you are on your honeymoon, be sure to tell everyone: flight attendants, waiters, hotel staff. They may throw in some extra perks and freebies.

IF YOU DON'T WANT TO BE DISTURBED by your friends or your family while you are on your honeymoon, be sure to register under a different name at the hotel. This is trickier than it used to be because they often ask to see ID now. But when I was first married they didn't. We registered under the name Mr. and Mrs. George Washington. When the desk clerk gave me a funny look, I told him I get that all the time. I assured him that I was not a descendant of the first president, but that I did have a picture of him in my wallet.

—*GEORGE SWAZUK*
FLORENCE, KENTUCKY
NUMBER OF WEDDING GUESTS: 100

I DON'T KNOW ONE GUY who got laid on his wedding night. And you know, we bitch about it over beer, but I wouldn't have wanted it any more than she did: I was drunk and exhausted. So what's wrong with snuggling on your wedding night? It's sweet. You've got the whole honeymoon for sex.

—*J.G.*
CHAPEL HILL, NORTH CAROLINA
NUMBER OF WEDDING GUESTS: 85

Have sex like it's the first time . . . even if it's not.

—*KIM SWIATEK*
WATTS FLATS,
NEW YORK
NUMBER OF WEDDING GUESTS: 200

DON'T SAVE MONEY BY SPENDING your first night together in your family home. I could hear my relatives talking and drinking late into the night. Not only did it put a damper on lovemaking, it also ruined any sleep we might have had. Finally, we just got up and joined them.

—*ANNE*
PARIS, FRANCE
NUMBER OF WEDDING GUESTS: 60

I DON'T THINK YOU WANT TO OVERDO IT. I didn't want to set some sexual tone for the marriage that would be unrealistic. If I had been hanging from the chandelier that night, wearing a see-through silk teddy, he might have gotten unrealistic expectations of the sex life to come. Stick to the basics.

—*DIANE COAN*
JAMESTOWN, NEW YORK
NUMBER OF WEDDING GUESTS: 100

MY HUSBAND AND I PUT FIVE DESTINATIONS in a hat and just picked one for our honeymoon, so there were no hard feelings about who chose where we went. It ended up being Maui, Hawaii, and it was one of the best weeks of my life.

—*SARAH MICKEY*
EVANSTON, ILLINOIS

REMEMBER, YOU ONLY GET one wedding night in your entire life so make the best of it. The key is to get as early a start as possible. Check out of the reception as early as you can without it seeming rude. Then head straight to the room. It helps if you can stay in the hotel where the reception is, as we did. My husband bought these little scented candles and put them everywhere in the room. Actually, there were too many, and it was too bright. So the first thing we did was to find this exciting way to go around, one by one, and put them out. The most important thing is to have fun, be creative, and go all night long.

—*ANONYMOUS*
GERRY, NEW YORK
NUMBER OF WEDDING GUESTS: 100

• • • • • • • •

YOU DON'T HAVE TO GO STRAIGHT from the wedding to the honeymoon. We did that, and we were so exhausted from the wedding weekend, we could barely find the energy to enjoy our honeymoon. Of course, we didn't have one of those relaxing-on-a-Hawaiian-beach kind of honeymoons; we went trekking in Nepal.

—*ELLEN*
KIRKLAND, WASHINGTON
NUMBER OF WEDDING GUESTS: 175

• • • • • • • •

DON'T LEAVE ON YOUR HONEYMOON until Tuesday if you are married on a Saturday. It was nice to have an easy Sunday with family and friends, go home and relax, and then spend Monday packing and running any last-minute errands before leaving on Tuesday morning. You also don't have the stress of packing for your honeymoon while trying to prepare for your wedding.

—*JOSH*
ST. PETERSBURG, FLORIDA
NUMBER OF WEDDING GUESTS: 250

By some accounts, honeymooning in Niagara Falls dates back to 1801, when the daughter of future vice president Aaron Burr traveled there with her fiancé.

TELL EVERYBODY YOU SEE THAT you're on your honeymoon—waiters, flight attendants, gate agents, hotel clerks, shop owners, you name it. You'll get lots of free deals, upgrades, and special little perks!

> —*ELLEN*
> *KIRKLAND, WASHINGTON*
> *NUMBER OF WEDDING GUESTS: 175*

· · · · · · · ·

" Anybody who's too burned out or too 'liberated' to get laid on his wedding night is pretty lame, and will have to live with that for the rest of his life. But I fear for a world in which having sex on your wedding night is no big deal. "

> —*ANONYMOUS*
> *BLUEFIELD, WEST VIRGINIA*
> *NUMBER OF WEDDING GUESTS: 175*

· · · · · · · ·

HER GRANDPARENTS OWNED some cabins near a beach, so we spent our honeymoon weekend there with both sets of parents. It was pretty cool—everybody had a really good time, and my wife and I still had plenty of alone time. Even better, including our parents reinforced strong family values from the beginning.

> —*ANTHONY MANUEL*
> *KINDER, LOUISIANA*
> *NUMBER OF WEDDING GUESTS: 20*

WE DIDN'T HAVE A GREAT DEAL OF MONEY and ended up car-camping through part of the Appalachian Trail for our honeymoon. We actually had a lovely, memorable time. If someone was really short on funds, loves the outdoors, and wanted to do something intimate, beautiful, and inexpensive, it is definitely one way to go.

—*CAROL*
EASTON, PENNSYLVANIA

. . . .

" As long as there's a comfy bed there, it doesn't really matter where you go. Most people don't leave their room for very long, anyway. "

—*SANDY JONES*
ZELIENOPLE, PENNSYLVANIA

. . . .

ONE LITTLE THING that I did that my wife really appreciated was suggest that we call her mom after we had been gone for about three days. She said later that she really wanted to call her mom, but she was afraid I'd get upset about it. I guess she figured my mother-in-law was the last person I'd want to talk to while we were away. But I suggested it and earned lots of points with both of them in the process.

—*J.D.*
WATTS FLATS, NEW YORK
NUMBER OF WEDDING GUESTS: 100

MAKE RESERVATIONS! My wife and I eloped and set off for our honeymoon in Saratoga Springs, New York. We didn't make reservations, figuring we'd just find a place to stay. As we drove, we noticed that none of the hotels along the way had vacancies! Turns out the World's Fair was in Canada that year, and every hotel room was booked, even 500 miles south of the border. In desperation, we stopped at a dilapidated hotel; the only one with a vacancy sign. It was such a firetrap, my wife and I slept in our clothes! The next day, my wife called the Saratoga Chamber of Commerce in tears, asking if they could help us find a place to stay. They found us a place at a brand new hotel. We had such a great time that we've gone back on vacations many times over the years.

—*J.B.*
ALLENTOWN, PENNSYLVANIA

Whipped cream: Don't leave home for a romantic getaway without it.

—*STEVEN KISTNER*
INDEPENDENCE, KENTUCKY
NUMBER OF WEDDING GUESTS: 100

* * * * * * * *

IF YOU'RE ADVENTUROUS, go on a honeymoon that can't be done once you've got kids or are retired. We went on an adrenaline-rush honeymoon to New Zealand. We bungee-jumped into our new life together.

—*K.R.*
SAN FRANCISCO, CALIFORNIA
NUMBER OF WEDDING GUESTS: 135

* * * * * * * *

MY HUSBAND AND I ARE BOTH DISNEY fanatics so picking a honeymoon spot was easy; we went to Disney World. Actually, we did the Disney cruise, where you spend some time at sea and some time on land in the park. It was wonderful. You want to be pampered on your honeymoon, and nobody knows how to spoil you rotten like Disney.

—*COLLEEN J.*
BULGER, PENNSYLVANIA
NUMBER OF WEDDING GUESTS: 200

FANTASY ISLAND

Maybe it's all the leis? Hawaii is the favorite honeymoon destination.

ANYTHING SHE WANTED—anything at all—I made sure she got. I wanted to pamper her as much as I could. We don't have tons of money and I knew that it might be the only time in our married life that I'd be able to do it. I spoiled her rotten. I think you have to make as much magic on your honeymoon as you can, because you never know when you'll have another chance to have such an experience.

> —*MICHAEL JOPLING*
> *GERRY, NEW YORK*
> *NUMBER OF WEDDING GUESTS: 175*

* * * * * * * *

REMEMBER THAT YOUR HONEYMOON is a vacation from planning your wedding, so don't do anything too complicated. If I had to plan anything after my wedding, such as where to go or what to do while I was on my honeymoon, I think my head would have exploded. All I wanted to do was lie on the beach.

> —*CARSON M.*
> *RALEIGH, NORTH CAROLINA*

* * * * * * * *

MY WIFE AND I WERE BOTH VIRGINS when we got married. If you save yourself for marriage, you must understand this: In the virgin groom's mind the only thing the honeymoon is for is sex, sex, and more sex. But, although the virgin bride will want to learn about sex as well, she's going to actually want to leave the hotel at some point. Unlike her new husband. We went to Florida and I couldn't have cared less if we were in the middle of Nebraska. I wasn't planning on seeing any of it. My wife, however, wanted to sightsee. We eventually reached a compromise.

> —*TOM BURDOCK*
> *POLAND, OHIO*
> *NUMBER OF WEDDING GUESTS: 75*

MY WIFE AND I WENT to Washington, D.C., for our honeymoon. We loved seeing all the wonderful sights there. The problem with D.C. as a honeymoon destination is that you tend to have to do a lot of walking. If you've only seen pictures of the Washington Mall you might mistakenly think that all of those attractions are close together; they're not. We did so much walking that at the end of the day we were almost too exhausted to do the normal honeymoon stuff in our hotel room. (I said *almost*.)

> —*TED VALKO*
> *CHURCHILL, OHIO*

Treat your spouse on the honeymoon like he/she is the sexiest person in the world. (When in doubt, keep refilling those Piña Coladas.)

> —*JENNIFER BRISMAN*
> *NEW YORK,*
> *NEW YORK*
> *NUMBER OF WEDDING GUESTS: 200*

THINGS CHANGE. Be OK with that and just enjoy whatever you end up doing as long as it is with your mate. My husband and I were married in Baton Rouge, Louisiana, at night and so we spent the wedding night in Biloxi, Mississippi, on our way to Florida for our honeymoon. At 2 a.m. on our wedding night we were awakened and made to evacuate because a hurricane had turned east and was heading our way. They would not let us drive toward Florida either, only west. So, we packed and headed to Texas. We had a great honeymoon in San Antonio. Twelve years later, we moved to San Antonio where we have resided ever since.

> —*CLAUDIA*
> *SAN ANTONIO, TEXAS*
> *NUMBER OF WEDDING GUESTS: 250*

HEAD LINES
Best Advice and Top Tips

- Take care of thank-you notes as soon as possible after you get back from your honeymoon.

- If you didn't live together before you were married, be prepared for a period of adjustment as you get used to each other's habits.

- Do something special together before you come down from the whole wedding experience and get back to your day-to-day lives.

- Savor the newness of being husband and wife for the first time for as long as you can.

DON'T HAVE YOUR GOWN PRESERVED. My gown sat in my closet for years until my husband surprised me by having it preserved. He knew how much it bothered me that I never had it done. As a special gift, he presented me with this beautiful box one Valentine's Day. I was brought to tears with his thoughtfulness. The tears flowed once again after I read articles about how people were charging to preserve these gowns when in actuality they were selling the gowns and putting rags in the box. After reading this I had to know, so I opened my box. To my horror I found what was similar to my gown but actually a shrunken, ruined piece of fabric. Pack your gown yourself in blue, acid-free tissue in an acid-free box, or keep it hanging to enjoy for years to come. Pass it on, but please don't have it preserved!

—*ANONYMOUS*
LONG VALLEY, NEW JERSEY

IF YOU'VE NEVER LIVED TOGETHER before the wedding, you'll need some time to adjust. It took me many, many months before I was not bothered by my husband's stuff taking over my dresser, even when it was neat and in his designated areas. I can still remember how much I resented his grubby socks. Now I couldn't live without them!

> —*MICHELLE*
> *SAN FRANCISCO, CALIFORNIA*

. . . .

"As soon as you get back from your honeymoon you should join a spa. I read somewhere that the average person gains 10 pounds on the honeymoon. You don't want to start down the road to Fat Town that early in a marriage."

> —*Z.E.*
> *NEW SPRINGFIELD, OHIO*
> *NUMBER OF WEDDING GUESTS: 250*

. . . .

WE MADE A POINT OF DOING the thank-you notes for each other's family and friends—I did those for the gifts from her side, she did them for my side. We felt it would establish credibility and a relationship with the other side. And we did them all within a week of getting the gift.

> —*ALLAN JAFFE*
> *PETALUMA, CALIFORNIA*
> *NUMBER OF WEDDING GUESTS: 90*

WEIRD WEDDING GIFTS

We take a break from these moments of bliss for a few rants and raves on the worst wedding gifts ever. It seems that weddings are the perfect time to give people things they don't need or can't use. So, as you unwrap the wagon-wheel coffee table from Uncle Billy, take heart: You are not alone.

WHAT I WOULD DEFINE AS RIDICULOUS GIFTS were all the checks that came addressed to Mr. and Mrs. Randy Rosenberg! First of all, I kept my name. And the assumption that money goes to him and the registry is mine is ridiculously offensive.

—MICHELLE ROTHSTEIN
TORONTO, ONTARIO, CANADA
NUMBER OF WEDDING GUESTS: 180

ONE PERSON GAVE US THE LARGEST DEVICE EVER made for opening a bottle of wine. It weighs about 15 pounds and it's three feet tall. It's massive, and it has to be mounted onto something. It's like a cast-iron Cuisinart. We feel bad getting rid of it, and we hope they don't come to visit because then we'd have to install it.

—ANONYMOUS
CAPE COD, MASSACHUSETTS
NUMBER OF WEDDING GUESTS: 150

THE WORST GIFT WE RECEIVED WAS A DONATION made in our name. We had never heard of the charity, the amount was never disclosed, and we never received a certificate from the charity. We got nothing—and we didn't even get to take the tax deduction!

—AMY
NEW YORK, NEW YORK

THE WORST GIFT WE RECEIVED WAS A PLAQUE with a prayer for the home on it. It was a $2.50 piece of garbage you'd see at Kmart. I couldn't imagine what we were going to do with this thing. When we opened the gift and I realized what it was, I was terrified that my wife might actually want to keep it. It was a reaffirming event when she didn't!

—*ANONYMOUS*
NEW YORK, NEW YORK
NUMBER OF WEDDING GUESTS: 200

THE WEIRDEST THING WE GOT was a $40 gift card to a local Wal-Mart-type store. I used it every day for a week to buy my lunch.

—*K.T.*
SEATTLE, WASHINGTON
NUMBER OF WEDDING GUESTS: 115

WE GOT MULTIPLE TOASTERS. We have to keep one of them and use it because it's from my husband's grandmother.

—*K.T.*
SEATTLE, WASHINGTON
NUMBER OF WEDDING GUESTS: 115

WE RECEIVED A PLATE WITH ALL OF OUR WEDDING DOCUMENTS and invitations put together on it like a collage. It was not really nice enough for our wall and we couldn't serve breakfast on it. It was very thoughtful, but quite impractical and ugly. And it smelled!

—*STEVE*
POTOMAC, MARYLAND

THE STRANGEST GIFT WE GOT was a set of Bart Simpson beach towels. We still have them 15 years later. Our kids use them.

> —*ANDREA COX*
> *GRAND LAKE, COLORADO*
> *NUMBER OF WEDDING GUESTS: 100*

● ● ● ● ● ● ● ●

THE WORST GIFT WE GOT WAS A SCALE. Who would give a bride a scale?!

> —*BECKY HOUK*
> *INDIANAPOLIS, INDIANA*
> *NUMBER OF WEDDING GUESTS: 300*

● ● ● ● ● ● ● ●

THE GIFT THAT TOOK THE CAKE FOR US: the Bed in a Bag. It's this ugly comforter set with hideous sheets and pillow shams, clearly re-gifted. We also got an old vegetable steamer that was re-gifted many times; we could tell because of all the tape marks on the box.

> —*JENIFER MANN*
> *CASTRO VALLEY, CALIFORNIA*
> *NUMBER OF WEDDING GUESTS: 35*

● ● ● ● ● ● ● ●

THE WEIRDEST GIFT WE GOT was a pregnant love goddess from Bali, which hangs on our lamp in the living room. Um, did we register for this?

> —*KALYNA*
> *SAN FRANCISCO, CALIFORNIA*
> *NUMBER OF WEDDING GUESTS: 120*

● ● ● ● ● ● ● ●

MY HUSBAND'S COUSIN GOT US A SHELL. Seriously. She wrote an elaborate note on it and even though it wasn't my style, I thought it was exotic. A few days later, I saw the shell in the air freshener aisle at the drugstore!

> —*ANONYMOUS*
> *NEW YORK, NEW YORK*
> *NUMBER OF WEDDING GUESTS: 105*

WE RECEIVED A TWO-FOOT-TALL METAL STATUE of a Chinese soldier from one of my friends. My wife and I were in a store a little while later and saw another one. So now we have two: They kind of just stand around in front of the fireplace and look menacing. You've got to have fun with stuff like that.

> —*T.K.*
> *NASHVILLE, TENNESSEE*

• • • • • • • •

SOME OF THE CRAZY STUFF YOU RECEIVE might actually grow on you. We received this weird tree—really, it was a tall tangle of vines in the shape of a thin Christmas tree. It even had tiny white lights on it. My wife's parents had to take it back to our house on the roof of their car while we went on our honeymoon. But the funny thing is, we still have the thing, 10 years later. It's like a part of the family now.

> —*J.A.*
> *ATLANTA, GEORGIA*
> *NUMBER OF WEDDING GUESTS: 200*

• • • • • • • •

A VIDEOTAPE OF *THE LAST WALTZ* and a record album entitled *The Worst Songs Ever Recorded;* from the same person.

> —*ANONYMOUS*
> *BROOKLYN, NEW YORK*
> *NUMBER OF WEDDING GUESTS: 70*

GET THE THANK-YOUS OUT as quickly as you can. Sending out the wedding thank-yous just wasn't high on our list of things to do. One day my mother-in-law called and said she had run into a friend of hers in the market. The friend had been at the wedding. The friend asked how the newlyweds were doing and how they had enjoyed the honeymoon. Then she said, "Boy they must be awful busy because I haven't gotten a thank-you yet."
Tacky, yes, but also effective. We started filling out the cards the next day.

—*MATT LAWTON*
HARRISONBURG, VIRGINIA

• • • • • • • •

THE NIGHT WE GOT BACK from our honeymoon, my husband crashed on the couch because he was so tired. I hid every single pair of his dress socks, which I knew he'd need for work the next day. It was so funny to watch him the next morning running around like a fool, looking for them. I had a hard time stifling my laughs. And it was even funnier when I saw him come home from work with athletic socks under his dress shoes. I was waiting for him in bed wearing nothing but a pair of his dress socks: I just wanted him to know that life with me was never going to be boring.

—*JULIA MORTON*
INDEPENDENCE, KENTUCKY
NUMBER OF WEDDING GUESTS: 200

RE-GIFTING, TWO DECADES LATER

We decided to return one of the five toasters we received to get something we could use. On returning it to Sears, the clerk had to call the manager: It appeared our model was not anywhere in the computer, it didn't come up under any other states, and it wasn't a model familiar to anyone who worked in the department. But the box clearly said "Sears" and it was never opened. The manager pulled out the dusty old reference books. He went back five years, 10 years, 15 years. Finally, they found it in the sales book from 20 years ago. It's amazing: That was the same year the gift-giver got married! All I could say was, "Well, hon, welcome to the family!" The manager was nice enough to give us today's value instead of what it would have cost to buy 20 years ago.

—ANONYMOUS
CLEVELAND, OHIO

HEADLINES
Best Advice and Top Tips

- Remember to be a guest at your own wedding—don't get so caught up in the details that you forget to have a good time.

- If you are changing your name, be sure to notify Social Security—once you receive your new card, it will be easier to change any other legal documents.

- Even in this day and age, *not* changing your name is a bigger deal than most people would think.

- Keep a wedding journal to remember everything about your special day—including all the planning that went into it.

I KEPT A JOURNAL OF EVERYTHING that happened, starting one week before the wedding and ending one week after. It doesn't have to be anything long: I just jotted down my thoughts. It's neat to look back at that now. There were certain things that I wrote down that I know I would have forgotten otherwise. You can even spruce the book up later with photos of the wedding: that's if you're really motivated.

—MARCY NUSSBAUMER
NEW ALBANY, OHIO

CHANGE YOUR NAME WITH SOCIAL SECURITY if you are taking your husband's name. It's very important. I kept putting it off and didn't actually make the change until about a year later. But when tax time came it caused me all kinds of problems.

—BEV TOLES
HARRISONBURG, VIRGINIA
NUMBER OF WEDDING GUESTS: 100

THE BIGGEST THING I HAVE LEARNED is that when you marry someone, you should accept them completely as they are. Don't expect them to change, and don't expect them to be perfect. I was not at all fooled by the time we got married, and I never thought, "Oh, he'll change this and that when we marry." He always accepted me completely as I was and I do the same for him.

—*PAULA EYERMAN*
DELAWARE, OHIO
NUMBER OF WEDDING GUESTS: 180

Be a guest at your wedding. Don't get caught up in whether or not the head table is facing twenty-five degrees to the north/north-west of the band, or if the flowers are the correct hue of magnolia blue. Nobody cares. Have fun!

—*L.S.*
SHARON,
MASSACHUSETTS

I DECIDED NOT TO CHANGE MY NAME, and it was a much bigger deal to a lot of people than I would have thought. People kept asking me, "Will you be offended if someone addresses an envelope to Mr. and Mrs. Stewart?" I guess not, but why not just use my name, too; is it that complicated? At least I was able to be honest about it, and it wasn't a big deal to my husband. I have a friend who never even told her in-laws that she kept her name. To this day, they think she's got a different name than she really does.

—*B.R.*
CHAPEL HILL, NORTH CAROLINA
NUMBER OF WEDDING GUESTS: 70

THE WEDDING IS THE PERFECT TIME to get a new family photo taken. We were going to get a picture with my parents and my brothers and sisters about a year before the wedding, but I suggested that we wait and do it during the wedding photo shoot. That way, everyone had the day already set aside, and they were dressed up. And it's cheaper because the bride and groom are already paying for the photographer's time.

—*BILL STUDENA*
FLORENCE, KENTUCKY
NUMBER OF WEDDING GUESTS: 100

WHEN MY HUSBAND AND I flew from California to Rome (where we were getting married), we managed to get upgraded to business class for free because I was carrying on my wedding dress (not something I wanted to risk losing in checked baggage). We got all the wine we wanted, and good edible food. My seat practically reclined into a bed. After the wedding, I left my dress with my mother in Rome to be cleaned. One day, when I'm in the mood to lug it back and want to try to get upgraded again, I'll bring it back to the United States.

—*M.B.*
WEEHAWKEN, NEW JERSEY
NUMBER OF WEDDING GUESTS: 70

INSTEAD OF STOWING ALL YOUR WEDDING CARDS away in a book, tuck them in little places all around the house, or under a beautiful dish or cake platter or other pretty things people have given you. Six months later, you'll pick up the cake platter and you'll think, "Oh, here's a card from my mom," and even if you've been fighting with your new spouse, you'll see this card that says how perfect you are for each other. It will make you feel good all over again. For months after the wedding, you'll be finding these cards that remind you that you really do want to be married to this person.

—*KAMI*
CAPE COD, MASSACHUSETTS
NUMBER OF WEDDING GUESTS: 150

CREDITS

Page 2: *www.Hallmark.com.*

Page 9: *www.CNN.com.*

Page 10: *Modern Bride* magazine and *Martha Stewart Weddings* magazine.

Page 12: *www.CNN.com.*

Page 28: *www.UltimateWedding.com.*

Page 38: *www.USABrides.com.*

Page 48: *Guinness Book of World Records.*

Page 56: *The New York Times* magazine, October 23, 2005.

Page 63: *Modern Bride* magazine.

Page 78: *Time* magazine, November 6, 1950.

Page 107: *www.Wikpedia.org.*

Page 113: *www.PoemsForFree.com.*

Page 122: *Time* magazine, October 3, 2005.

Page 131: Compiled from *www.FrugalWedding.com* and *www.UltimateWedding.com.*

Page 150: *Guiness Book of World Records.*

Page 151: *www.Hallmark.com.*

Page 160: *Wedding* magazine.

Page 164: The Wedding Channel.

Page 166: "New York Wedding Guide," *New York* magazine, Fall 2005.

Page 169: *Wedding* magazine and *www.ThePerfectToast.com.*

Page 180: "Niagra Falls: Honeymoon Central," Canada for Visitors, *www.About.com.*

Page 188: *www.Hallmark.com.*

HELP YOUR FRIENDS SURVIVE!

Order extra copies of *Where to Seat Aunt Edna* or one of our other books.

Please send me:

_____ copies of *Where to Seat Aunt Edna* (@$13.95)

_____ copies of *"You Can Keep the Damn China!"* (@$13.95)

_____ copies of *How to Lose 9,000 Lbs. (or Less)* (@$13.95)

_____ copies of *How to Survive Your Teenager* (@$13.95)

_____ copies of *How to Survive a Move* (@$13.95)

_____ copies of *How to Survive Your Marriage* (@$13.95)

_____ copies of *How to Survive Your Baby's First Year* (@$12.95)

_____ copies of *How to Survive Dating* (@$12.95)

_____ copies of *How to Survive Your Freshman Year* (@$13.95)

Please add $3.00 for shipping and handling for one book, and $1.00 for each additional book. Georgia residents add 4% sales tax. Kansas residents add 5.3% sales tax. Payment must accompany orders. Please allow three weeks for delivery.

My check for $_____ is enclosed.

Please charge my __ Visa __ MasterCard __ American Express

Name _____

Organization _____

Address _____

City/State/Zip _____

Phone _____E-mail _____

Credit card # _____

Exp. Date _____Signature _____

Please make checks payable to: HUNDREDS OF HEADS BOOKS, LLC
#230
2221 PEACHTREE ROAD, SUITE D
ATLANTA, GA 30309

VISIT WWW.HUNDREDSOFHEADS.COM

Do you have something interesting to say about marriage, your in-laws, dieting, holding a job, or one of life's other challenges?

Help humanity—share your story!

 Get published in our next book!

 Find out about the upcoming titles in the HUNDREDS OF HEADS™ survival guide series!

 Read up-to-the-minute advice on many of life's challenges!

 Sign up to become an interviewer for one of the next HUNDREDS OF HEADS® survival guides!

Visit www.hundredsofheads.com today!

About the Editors

HARRIETTE ROSE KATZ founded Gourmet Advisory Services, Inc. in 1979 and Liaison Unlimited ten years later, combining her passion for the culinary arts with her extensive global travel to form a company renowned in the New York metropolitan area. Harriette and her expert staff have designed, created, and managed thousands of events, including the weddings of celebrities and the openings of luxury high-rise office and residential buildings.

Harriette served for sixteen years as the President and Chief Operating Officer, New York Chapter of the Confrerie de la Chaine Des Rotisseurs, one of the world's most prestigious food and wine organizations, and is a recipient of the Chaine's Gold Star of Excellence. In addition, she is a member of the L'Ordre Mondial des Gourmet Degustateurs, and The Wine and Food Society of New York.

BESHA RODELL is a writer and award-winning journalist, with articles in many newspapers and magazines. She lives in Chapel Hill, North Carolina.

Besha has been to over 20 weddings in the past two years. She has seen friends and family driven to madness by their own weddings, and vowed not to let this happen to her. In the summer of 2005, she organized her own wedding without hiring one single person—not a florist, caterer, or photographer. She did it all herself with the help of a couple of friends, had a wonderful wedding day, and lived to tell the tale.